101 Things

You Didn't Know about

THE MAFIA

The lowdown on dons, wiseguys, squealers, and backstabbers

James Mannion

Adams Media
Avon, Massachusetts

Published by Adams Media, an F+W Publications Company
57 Littlefield Street, Avon, MA 02322
www.adamsmedia.com.

ISBN: 1-59337-267-1
Printed in Canada
J I H G F E D C B A

Library of Congress Cataloging-in-Publication Data
Mannion, James.
101 things you didn't know about the Mafia / by James Mannion.
p.   cm.
ISBN 1-59337-267-1
1. Mafia—Italy. 2. Mafia—United States. 3. Organized crime—Italy. 4. Organized crime—United States. 5. Mafia. I. Title: One hundred one things you didn't know about the Mafia. II. Title: One hundred and one things you didn't know about the Mafia. III. Title.
HV6453.I83M3568 2005
364.1'06'0973—dc22

2004019230

Contains portions of material adapted and abridged from *The Everything® Mafia Book* by James Mannion, ©2003, Adams Media Corporation.

This book is available at quantity discounts for bulk purchases.
For information, please call 1-800-872-5627.

Contents

Introduction

Just about everybody knows something about the Mafia. It has fascinated people since it was brought out of the shadowy underworld and into the light. People followed the stories of gangland slayings and fierce Tommy gun battles during the Roaring '20s, when the Mafia came to national prominence. Some chose to view the Mafia as flawed heroes—modern-day Robin Hoods who bucked the system and gave the people what they wanted, and what the government tried to deny them of during Prohibition—a good, stiff drink. But there's more to the Mafia's story than just bootleg moonshine—the organization was and is far more dangerous than that.

From the Roaring '20s through the comparatively boring '80s, the Mafia continued to enthrall the public. The '20s had Al Capone; the '80s gave us the "Teflon Don," John Gotti. Too many folks regarded them as appealing mavericks, but make no mistake: They were stone-cold killers who made a nice living by stealing things from other people.

Today, almost everyone is familiar with the *Godfather* movies, the films of Martin Scorsese, and the television show *The Sopranos*. We live in an age where Mafia kingpins write their memoirs and low-level leg breakers write cookbooks. People know that these mobsters are killers, but they regard them as entertaining oddities. Because, for the most part, Mafiosi only kill their own, average Joes can safely enjoy their antics from a discreet distance and live vicariously through their melodrama.

101 Things You Didn't Know about the Mafia will introduce you to aspects of Mafia history, mystery, and lore that will probably be new to you. You will learn some tidbits and trivia that only a hardcore Mafia junkie may know. An amateur expert on all things Mafia may not find too many surprises here, but this is not a book for the experts. This is a book for people with a casual knowledge but deeper interest in the Mafia's amazing and violent tales. Some of the names and events will be familiar; others you will be learning about for the first time.

Did you know that Al Capone had a long-lost brother who was a lawman at the same time that Al was the crime king of Chicago? You probably have heard of Eliot Ness, but how about Elmer Irey, the accountant who was instrumental in bringing down Capone? And maybe you know a little something about John Gotti, head of the Gambino crime family in New York City, but does the name Carlo Caputo ring a bell? Caputo and another guy formed a two-man crime family operating out of Madison, Wisconsin. And how did Desi Arnaz end up crossing paths with the Mafia? Arnaz regularly told his wife, Lucy, that she had some "'splainin'" to do, but *he* was the one who had to do some 'splainin' to the Mafia when he produced the hit television show *The Untouchables*.

These tidbits are just the start. *101 Things You Didn't Know about the Mafia* will give you a seldom-seen peek at the world of organized crime. You'll learn all sorts of things you didn't know as you enrich your understanding of the Mafia's fascinating and deadly world.

Crime has been around since the dawn of humankind, and organized crime has been around almost as long. Ever since humans, social animals by nature, banded together in primitive tribal associations, there have been rogue elements that also banded together in the shadows to prey on the rest of the pack. And as long as there have been societies, there have been secret societies within them. Many of these secret societies had a criminal element.

Rather than put in an honest day's labor to earn their living, these devious derelicts thought it was a better arrangement to steal from the hard-working members of their society instead.

Part 1

Prehistory

Out of these criminal factions, the Mafia was born. There are different theories about the Mafia's origins and how the organization got its name. Those who associate the Mafia with the crime syndicates that flourished in the Roaring '20s and continue—albeit in a less flamboyant manner—to operate up to and includ-

The Sicilian Vespers

There are many theories and legends about how the Mafia began. One of them involves a revolution in Sicily way back in 1282 that has come to be known as "the Sicilian Vespers." At this time, the French king Charles I took over Sicily with the blessing of the Pope in Rome. This was an age when, in addition to its spiritual control over Europe, the Vatican also wielded enormous secular power and influence. During the Middle Ages, the Jewish people were a minority without a homeland, Islam remained in the Middle East, and the Protestant Reformation was still a couple of hundred years away. The Catholic Church was a monopoly, and its edicts made monarchs toe the line, lest they risk excommunication and its attendant damnation.

Legend has it that the Sicilian citizenry rose up in rebellion after an incident during evening vespers, a prayer service in Catholic tradition. One particular evening, a Sicilian woman went to church looking for her daughter, who left home after telling her mother she would be there all day in solemn prayer and devotion. The woman arrived to find the daughter being raped in the sacred space by a French soldier. She ran through the streets, screaming, "My daughter, my daughter!" in a medieval Sicilian dialect of that time, which was "*Ma fia, ma fia!*"

Mafia. Get it?

In other historical accounts, the young woman is not raped, but merely "insulted" by a French soldier. Perhaps this was one historian's attempt to clean things up a little, but it serves as further evidence that historical accounts can be very subjective, indeed. The point is, writers' biases often come through in historical accounts, and many times, writers add their own spin to the telling of the tale, which makes their tales inherently suspect. (The old cliché that history is written by the conquerors is all too true.) Case in point: A Mafioso's written account of his own life would be markedly different than the same story told by the lawman intent on bringing him down.

Nevertheless, in the case of this story, the incident sparked a violent insurrection by the Sicilian people against the French occupying force. In about six weeks, more than 8,000 French soldiers had been massacred, and the rest fled the island. Lest you think this led to the liberation of the Sicilian people, they were not so fortunate. Sicily's history is nothing but a lengthy list of conquests, and the unfortunate island wasn't left alone for long. The Spanish quickly took advantage of the chaos that ensued during this rebellion, and they set up shop as the French were being shown the door.

Sicily's history continued to be one of occupation, but an underground movement was born, and many believe that was the Mafia's genesis.

Omerta: The code of silence

The Mafia ritual called *omerta* originated in Sicily. It is translated as "manhood," but the term has evolved into the Mafia's code of silence. Rituals of initiation into manhood have existed in every culture going back to ancient and primitive societies. These rites of passage often involved elaborate ceremonies. In keeping with those sorts of traditions, the Mafia shrouds its activities with pomp and circumstance to give them an air of dignity. These rituals are an amalgam of Roman Catholic, Freemason, and native Sicilian traditions.

Omerta is part of the modern Mafia's tradition of being "made," that is, allowing members into the inner sanctum of the Mafia family. The cost of this membership doesn't come cheap. Before being admitted into the inner sanctum, a would-be member must first kill someone or participate in a murder, even if the initiate isn't the one who pulls the trigger.

Along with the vow of omerta, another element of the Mafia code is a vow of total devotion and loyalty to the head of the family, or don. This practice comes from the ancient traditions of royalty and the divine right of kings. By declaring it was God's will that they be on the throne, the clever kings maneuvered around challenges to their rule.

Another source of this Mafia tradition of total obedience to the don is the feudal system. In this medieval social structure, a feudal lord in his castle lorded over the peasant class. Serfs, as the peasants were called, worked the land and delivered the majority of the produce to the castle while they kept just enough for themselves to eat. This medieval tradition is carried on in the modern Mafia, where the people on the lower rungs of the hierarchy work for the good of those above them.

The Sicilian Mafia's code also includes the duty to offer help to anyone "in the family"—that is, any person or group with close ties to the Mafia—who needs assistance. The fierce loyalty to all friends and equally fierce hostility to any outsiders is a cornerstone of both the Old-World and New-World Mafia.

The Sicilian Mafia also has an edict insisting that its members avoid interaction with the authorities. They can bribe corrupt police-men and crooked politicians, even intimidate and kill them, but they are not allowed to socialize with them.

The Camorra

The Camorra is the secret criminal society of Naples. It predates the modern Mafia and now exists concurrently with the Mafia. Its main enterprises included robbery, blackmail, and murder. Although its origins are vague, some speculate the Camorra was a criminal organization imported from Spain. (The word *camorra* means "quarrel" in Spanish.) The first mention of the Camorra in written accounts dates back to 1820. Membership is believed to have spread in the prisons of Naples. Prisons have always been hotbeds of discord, and men and women often emerge from them anything but rehabilitated. In this instance, the Bourbon French, who controlled Naples at the time, unfairly imprisoned many individuals, and the Camorra was a prison subculture that attracted many political prisoners, and just plain bad guys as well.

The Camorra came into public view when those who joined its ranks were gradually released from jail in the 1830s. It began as little more than a confederation of street gangs. These gangs had a unique system of communication on those dark and narrow streets of Naples. They signaled one another by making animal noises. A "meow" meant the cops were coming, and crowing like a rooster indicated a potential mugging victim was approaching. As the society grew in power and prestige, it branched out into more ambitious criminal activities such as smuggling, prostitution, and a numbers racket. Soon, the Camorra worked hand in glove with the corrupt princes and politicians of the day.

Just like the Mafia, the Camorra had a hierarchal structure and several levels of membership. There were the elites and the low-level soldiers, and twelve "chiefs" operated under one supreme chief. These chiefs were the equivalent of Mafia dons and the "boss of bosses."

Unlike the Mafia, however, the rank and file elected the chiefs, kind of like a trade union.

A man was initiated into the Camorra in a unique way. A gold coin was tossed on the ground and the initiate had to grab it while several gang members thrust their daggers at the coin. Few initiates passed this test of courage and character without suffering a few cuts and gashes in the process.

During the nineteenth century, Naples was a chaotic, lawless town—a perfect place for a criminal underground to thrive. Ironically, for all the Camorra did to contribute to that lawlessness, it also actually helped the police to solve some crimes. The Camorra even became a political party in 1848, the year when the Italian city-states were unified into one nation under the Tuscan sun. From that point on, the Camorra became an entrenched fact of Neapolitan society. Its members were involved in government, the bureaucracy, and law enforcement.

However, there were reformers who sought to eradicate the Camorra. In 1877, fifty-seven members were arrested in one fell swoop, and by 1901 a group called the Honest Government defeated the last of the "legitimate" Camorra members in an election. Members of the Camorra were ousted from the light, but like Mafiosi, they thrived in darkness.

Mussolini cracked down on the Camorra when he came to power in 1922, and it was largely immobilized during his fascist reign. But like the Sicilian Mafia, the Camorra benefited from America's victory during World War II—it's far easier for a criminal organization to thrive in a democracy than in a dictatorship. This criminal organization still exists today.

Southern-fried scandal

People usually associate the Mafia with the Roaring '20s and the rat-a-tat-tat of Tommy guns in Chicago or New York. But the word *Mafia* actually came into national consciousness in 1891 in the Deep South. In the 1860s, a wave of immigrants came to America from Italy and Sicily. More immigrants came, in even greater numbers, in the 1890s. In the first wave, thousands of Italians and Sicilians settled in New Orleans, Louisiana. It was in this Southern port city that the first official Mafiosi took up where they left off in their native land. Yes, New Orleans, not New York or Chicago, was the real birthplace of the modern American Mafia.

These Louisiana Mafia gangs were using Sicilian Mafia techniques to extort money from their own kinsmen. For example, a politely written note would be left for a merchant or businessman, stating that money was expected at a certain date/time or the letter recipient would be brutally killed. The bizarre Old-World gentility of the letter's wording contrasted with the threats of violence. But this was no bluff. People really were beaten, businesses were trashed, and families were killed if they did not make a prompt payment to the sender. The only signature on these letters was a black palm print—hence the name Black Hand for the Mafia. The numerous clans committed more than 100 killings in New Orleans, during the wave of immigration from the 1860s through the 1890s.

At this time, the mayor of New Orleans was a man named Shakespeare. He did not like the wave of Sicilian immigration and spoke against his new neighbors in no uncertain terms. He called the Italian newcomers "vicious and worthless," adding that they were "without courage, honor, truth, pride, religion, or any quality that goes to make good citizens." He went even further by threatening "to put an end to these infernal Dago disturbances, even if it proves necessary to wipe out every one of you from the face of the earth." Strong stuff indeed, but the actions of the Mafia were tarnishing the image of all Sicilians, including those upstanding citizens who had nothing to do with organized crime. The Mafia is bad news in any city, but the New Orleans Mafia was particularly vicious, which only made matters worse.

New Orleans Police Chief David Peter Hennessey was determined to put an end to Mafia activity in his city. He spoke to some of the Sicilian immigrants and learned that even the nongangsters were inclined to be insular and clannish. They still retained their innate Old-World distrust of authority. Most would not talk to him, but those who did whispered an alien phrase that, up to that point, had not been uttered before on American soil—*La Mafia*. That was when Hennessey discovered the existence of a secret organized collective of criminals. He was dealing with something deeper and more menacing than mere street hoodlums.

After gleaning this knowledge, Hennessey became a marked man. The Mafia followed him and noted his routine. A hit was in the works.

Hennessey was brave but foolish. He could not be bribed, and he remained unfazed by the many death threats he received. He meticulously built a case against the Mafia gang leaders called the Matranga brothers. Right about the time he was ready to present his airtight case to a grand jury, four men on a darkened street crept up and surrounded him. All four men brandished shotguns and fired at close range.

Even though he was cut to ribbons, Hennessey fired in vain at his murderers and then dragged himself back to the police station. His friend Captain Billy O'Connor and another policeman discovered him. O'Connor asked Hennessey if he knew who had shot him, and Hennessey uttered a sentence that unleashed a wave of violence and retribution and achieved national attention: "The Dagos did it." (*Dago* is an ethnic slur for an Italian—although it is not very common today, for many decades, it was used quite liberally.)

The actual culprits were rounded up in the dragnet, but so were many other innocent men. After they were all thrown in the slammer, an informant in the jail got cozy with one of the accused, who spilled the beans about the conspiracy against Hennessey. The loose-lipped prisoner implicated high-level members of the Matranga clan, including Charles Matranga, Joe Macheca, and numerous others. The trial divided the country along ethnic lines. The Mafia, in turn, exploited ethnic pride to collect money for a defense fund for the accused.

Nineteen Sicilian men were brought to trial for the murder of Police Chief Hennessey, but in a story that quickly became a tried-and-true Mafia trick, the local gangsters bribed and intimidated the witnesses and the jury. The frightened jurors found sixteen of the accused not guilty. They couldn't come to a verdict on the other three, including the two kingpins, Matranga and Macheca, who would have to stand trial again.

The jury verdicts sparked uproar in the city of New Orleans. Eight thousand people assembled at the city hall. They listened to inflammatory rhetoric from several notable citizens, one of whom flat out exhorted the throng to take the law into its own hands. The crowd raided the city armory and proceeded to the prison where the Mafiosi were being held. The prison warden let the Italians out of their cells so the rioters could get to them.

The angry mob barreled into the prison looking for the Mafiosi. Top man Joseph Macheca was shot dead. The crowd also rounded up and shot six others. Another, Manuel Polizzi, was dragged from the prison and lynched. Several members of the lynch mob shot him as he writhed at the end of the rope. A total of sixteen men were killed that day. Two of them had no mob connections at all. They were executed simply for being Sicilian. In a stroke of luck for the Mafia, its leader, Charles Matranga, the man who had orchestrated the murder of the police chief, survived the mob's bloodlust. He was able to hide successfully and escape the carnage.

The newspapers ran editorials in support of the vigilante murders. One paper lauded the crazed mob for its self-control, reporting that only the Mafiosi were killed, which was not at all true. The episode soon mushroomed into an international incident. The Italian ambassador lodged a complaint with President Benjamin Harrison, as did the Italian government. Rumors of a potential war between the United States and Italy filled the newspapers. Harrison denounced the incident, and the government paid settlements to the families of the murder victims. None of the vigilante mob or the men who incited them were brought to trial, however. All charges against Mafia kingpin Charles Matranga were ultimately dismissed, and he laid low after that. The lion's share of the $25,000 sent to the families of the victims ended up in the Mafia's coffers. After the massacre, the newspapers announced that the Mafia was dead and buried. But, of course, the press was dead wrong.

Spaghetti Western

The Denver crime family began its activity in the 1880s, and the ensuing events played out more like a Western movie than a gangster melodrama. The exploits of this crime family just go to show that the Mafia is not just an urban phenomenon. The Mafia took its rough and rowdy antics everywhere, and mob activity could be found all over the country, including the so-called Wild West.

The first boss of the Denver mob was a French Canadian named Lou Blonger. He ran saloons that also featured prostitution as an attraction. This was common in the Old West. Blonger and his brother were involved in the usual vices: gambling, prostitution, and so on. He also monitored newcomers in town. If you were a journeyman pickpocket or a penny-ante grifter, you had to drop by Blonger's office to ask permission and make payment arrangements for the privilege of doing business in Denver. All this criminality went on under the watchful eye and complicity of the police department. Corruption ran rampant in the force.

Blonger's career lasted from the wild and woolly 1880s until the 1920s, when he was finally imprisoned. He was an old man at the time and died five months into his ten-year sentence.

During the 1920s, in an effort to counter the mob violence in

Denver, the citizenry turned to an equally unsavory organization, the Ku Klux Klan, to restore order. Many cops, including the chief of police, were Klansmen. The KKK did not vanquish vice in Denver, however, it simply controlled and profited from it. The mayor during this time, although elected with support from the Klan, eventually had enough of the group's hypocrisy and corruption. He deputized 125 members of the American Legion, took on the Klan, and won, eliminating the KKK's influence in the police force.

Meanwhile, the Italians arrived in Colorado during the 1930s, in the persons of Pete and Sam Carlino. These guys meant business—the former being dubbed "the Al Capone of Colorado." Gang wars that rivaled those in Chicago followed, with the Carlinos battling another Mafioso, Joe Roma, for control of Denver's lucrative bootlegging business. Peter Carlino survived an attempted hit by the Roma gang in 1930, and in 1931, Roma bailed him out of jail after being arrested on an arson charge. Either Roma wanted Carlino on the street where he was an easier target, or he was afraid he might sing while in the slammer. Or maybe it was just another instance of the American Mafia wanting to keep its battles in the family.

Pete Carlino would probably have lived longer had he stayed behind bars. His bullet-riddled body was dumped under a bridge shortly thereafter. When it remained undiscovered for a couple of days, the killers retrieved it and placed it in a more public location. Carlino's brother got whacked a little while later, and the five-foot-one Roma became the crime boss of Denver. But not for long. "Little Caesar," as he was known, was murdered in 1933.

Talk to the Hand

The America Mafia has its origins on the island of Sicily, which is off the coast of Italy in the Mediterranean Sea. The island has had a tumultuous history that has proved to be fertile soil for an underworld crime structure to take root.

Sicily's history is one of occupation. The native inhabitants were called Siculi, and it is believed that they came over to the island from southern Italy during the mists of prehistory, before the time when written records were chiseled into stone or scratched onto papyrus. Hence, we do not know the exact date this band of travelers set sail from the mainland.

These Siculi, sometimes called the Sicani, were subject to the whims and fancies of invading forces from day one. First it was the Greeks and Phoenicians who took up residence. Next came the Carthaginians, who arrived on the island and waged war with the Greeks for supremacy. These groups battled it out for many decades, and control changed hands more than once.

Then, the mighty Romans came, saw, and conquered. In A.D. 440, the barbarian tribe called the Vandals conquered Sicily. These Vandals did more than scrawl graffiti on the walls. They were a barbarian horde that raped, pillaged, and ravaged the land after the Roman Empire collapsed. Then it was the Byzantine Empire's turn. The Saracens, a group of Arabs who practiced the newly established religion of Islam, attacked and occupied the island in 827.

Next, the Norman French ousted the Arabs after a thirty-year war that ended in 1091. In 1194, the House of Hohenstaufen, part of the Holy Roman Empire, invaded, conquered, and occupied Sicily for a time. During the late Middle Ages and the Renaissance, the Spanish and French were also in control of the island for various periods of time.

The point is, native Sicilians, who came over from Italy before recorded history, never had control of their island homeland. Millennia of subjugation made the people insular, clannish, and suspicious. This climate allowed the secret society that became the Mafia to germinate and grow.

By the 1700s, the Mafia had begun to extort money from the very people it purported to protect. People would receive courtly and politely written letters "requesting" money for protection. The gimmick was that the money was protection from the group that sent the letter. If the recipient did not pay up, they could expect a violent response. People lived in terror that one of these notes would be slipped under their door.

Family members might be kidnapped and held for ransom. Their houses could be set ablaze and destroyed. They might even be killed.

The Black Hand terrorized Sicilians for decades, and when the Mafia made its way to the New World, the Black Hand tradition continued in the land of the free and the home of the brave.

The case of the terrorized tenor

The precursor of the Mafia, known as the Black Hand, thrived in America in the nineteenth and early twentieth centuries, just as it had in Sicily for centuries. During that time, members of the Black Hand successfully extorted money from many citizens, mostly their fellow Italian immigrants. The Black Hand did not discriminate based on socioeconomic standing. The poor and the rich were terrorized with equal vigor. The small shopkeeper was victimized, and so was one of the most famous celebrities of the day, the opera star Enrico Caruso.

Caruso, who was born in Naples, Italy, in 1873, rose from very humble beginnings to reach the pinnacle of his profession. He was internationally known as the greatest opera singer of the time, and back then, his fame gave him an exalted status much like that of a rock star today. Coming from a poor Neapolitan upbringing, he was, no doubt, aware of the Black Hand—and for good reason.

In the early 1900s, Caruso received a letter with the telltale black hand imprinted upon it. According to this letter, Caruso's golden throat would be cut if he did not pay up. Understandably, Caruso was terrified, and so he contacted his friend Joe Petrosini, the hero-cop and leader of the New York City Police Department's "Italian Squad," which was waging war on the Mafia. Although the opera singer arranged to make the payment, Joe Petrosini was there in his stead. Petrosini was a genuine straight arrow—an honest, by-the-book cop. But in this case, he made an exception. When the gangster appeared to collect his loot, Petrosini broke both his legs, took him directly to a ship heading to Sicily, and assured him that he would be killed if he ever came back to America. (Years later, the Caruso/Petrosini incident was dramatized in the 1960 movie *Pay or Die*. Ernest Borgnine played Joe Petrosini.)

Although quite out of character for Petrosini, his daring move, with all the visceral appeal of Dirty Harry, achieved the desired result. This story raises an interesting and controversial point. If this type of strategy had been used on all Mafiosi from day one, would they have still become so firmly enmeshed in the American culture? Of course, this is a loaded question. Police vigilantism might lead to a police state—something only a dictator would want. Broader political implications aside, the fact remains Petrosini broke the rules (and the legs) to protect his friend from the wrath of the Black Hand, and to send the members of the group a message they would not forget. Ironically, although Petrosini won the upper hand in this round, several years later, in 1909, the Mafia actually gunned him down.

"Piddu" Morello: The first American Mafioso

Giuseppe "Joe" Morello is the first American gangster to be identified by the authorities as the head of the Mafia in America. He was actually a co-leader of the Black Hand (his fellow coleader being Lupo Saietta). If you sketch out a family tree of the Mafia in America, this branch of the Black Hand did, through serpentine twists and turns, from the late nineteenth century through the 1930s, evolve into what became the Genovese crime family after Lucky Luciano and friends refined the organized crime into the modern Mafia.

Morello was part of a large extended family, and they were all Mafiosi. This crime family really was a family.

Joe Morello was a main player in the early twentieth century battle between the Black Hand in New York and hero-cop Joe Petrosini, which is reported elsewhere in this book. Petrosini was murdered in 1909, and then in 1910, Morello and Saietta were found guilty of counterfeiting and sent up the river for thirty years. They were paroled after only ten, and by then the torch had been passed to the next generation of the Morello gang.

The Morello family was a part of the Mafia known as the Mustache Petes, stuffy Old-World hoodlums who did not embrace the American way. They were ultimately usurped by Joe "The Boss" Masseria who was, in turn, deposed by Lucky Luciano.

Joe The Boss was New York's answer to Al Capone during the 1920s. He left his native Sicily with a price on his head, first seeing Lady Liberty in New York Harbor in 1903. He went to work for the Morello gang on Manhattan's Lower East Side, where his singular talents as an enforcer were in great demand.

Future Mafia dons are nothing if not ambitious. It was not long before Masseria grew tired of being somebody else's leg breaker. The Mustache Pete syndrome got its first kick in the pants when Masseria and a few loyal confederates attacked the Morello gang's headquarters and killed several loyalists. Morello carried out additional hits until the hoods decided it was better to switch sides than fight, and so they consolidated under his leadership. Masseria was then the boss of bosses of New York City. If he could make it there, he could make it anywhere.

Thanks to his ability to survive multiple assassination attempts, Masseria gained a reputation as something of a supergangster. One of the first hits on Masseria was ordered by a certain Signore Morello, the guy who had his gang shot out from under him. In this legendary near-hit, Masseria's two bodyguards were shot dead as they flanked him on the sidewalks of New York, but hit man Umberto Valenti missed Mr. Big. Valenti chased Masseria into a shop, firing ten shots that the Boss successfully dodged. This feat earned Masseria a reputation for being "bulletproof." No bad deed went unpunished, and Valenti was later whacked on the orders of Masseria. A pragmatic hood, Masseria accepted the olive branch from Morello and even made him one of his lieutenants.

The Ndrangheta

This unusual Greek word is sometimes translated as "heroism" or "virtue." It is also the name for an Italian crime family that originated in the Italian province of Calabria. Sometimes called the Calabrian Mafia simply because it is a criminal organization of Italian origin, the Ndrangheta developed because of many of the same issues that prompted the rise of the Sicilian Mafia—particularly because of the local folks' distrust of the never-ending succession of invaders who attacked Italy. The Ndrangheta is also referred to as L'Onorata Societa (The Honorable Society) and La Famiglia (The Family). However you slice it, the

Ndrangheta is believed to be older than what we know as the Mafia, and it still exists today.

The organization was and is structurally different from the Mafia. In the Ndrangheta, literal familial relationships and towns of origin linked crime families. Although Mafiosi often talk about "family," this does not necessarily mean a literal family. In the early days it did, but over time that changed, and the American Mafia families became more like businesses than insular clans. Like the Mafia, the Ndrangheta spread from Italy to other lands, including Germany, Eastern Europe, Canada, Australia, several countries in South America, and the United States.

Beyond the typical Mafia enterprises of extortion, drugs, and so on, nowadays, the Ndrangheta organization is also involved in an international weapons trafficking business that is quite lucrative in this age of terrorism. Members of the Ndrangheta are indiscriminate about their clientele. They would have no compunction about dealing with groups whose stated mandate is the destruction of the Western World. This makes the Ndrangheta and other contemporary Mafiosi far more malevolent than their forebears.

In other aspects of its business, the Ndrangheta deals with rural rather than urban crime.

Just as a Mafia family in a city would try to extort protection money from businesses, large and small, and attempt to entrench itself in enterprises like waste management, the Ndrangheta does the same thing to agricultural communities in Italy. Farmers pay for the protection of their crops and others are intimated into selling the family farm for a nominal sum so as to avoid being murdered. When the Ndrangheta takes over a farm and sends its agrarian goon squad in to run it, it's almost a sure shot that the crop they grow will be marijuana.

Members of the Ndrangheta also have interest in the wholesale food business. Chances are this nefarious group is making a profit on the next bottle of imported olive oil that you purchase from the market. It has also been accused of illegally dumping radioactive waste in the Italian countryside. The Ndrangheta is doing this for other parties, probably businesses and industries, and perhaps even rogue governments that want to sidestep the many necessary safety regulations surrounding the disposal of toxic waste.

The Ndrangheta, unlike the violent fictitious Corleone gang of Sicily, does not engage in violent conflict with the police and other law enforcement or governmental bodies. It prefers to remain in the darkness, using threats and bribery to encourage the authorities to cooperate or at least turn a blind eye to its activities.

10

Pet shop boy: Monk Eastman

Before the Mafia became a pop-culture phenomenon, there were the gangs of New York. These gangs were made up of the vast melting pot of immigrants who came to America in the nineteenth century. One of the most notorious was the Eastman gang from Manhattan's Lower East Side.

The gang's leader was Monk Eastman. Born Edward Osterman in 1873, he was the son of Jewish immigrants. Like many a crime family, the Eastmans started out as little more than a street gang. They were muggers and heist men before graduating to prostitution and other criminal enterprises.

The belief that Hitler loved dogs applies to this Jewish killer as well. One of Eastman's legitimate business fronts was a pet shop, and he eventually became so devoted to his merchandise that he kept the entire store of cats and birds as his personal pets. He conducted mob business with a cat in his lap, like James Bond's nemesis Ernest Stavro Blofeld, and a bird on his shoulder, just like *Treasure Island's* Long John Silver.

While fond of furry creatures, he was less kind to the human animal. He liked to crack people over the head with a baseball bat, and he would carve a notch on the bat for every head. It is even alleged that he whacked a guy upside the head for no other reason than to make the number of notches an even fifty.

Eastman's gang had a price list for each of its activities: $15 to beat someone up, $25 to stab a person, and $100 to kill them. These are nineteenth-century prices, of course. Just imagine what inflation would do to these rates today.

The Eastman gang had more than 1,200 members at its height, and members actually worked for the New York City mayor, the famously corrupt "Boss" Tweed. They made sure people "voted early and voted often" for Tweed and his cronies. In turn, although gang members were frequently arrested, they were rarely convicted.

The Eastmans' main rivals were the Italian Five Points gang. In the early twentieth century, they vied for the Lower East Side of Manhattan, the same territory featured in the Martin Scorsese movie *Gangs of New York*. Monk Eastman survived an assassination attempt in 1901. This culminated in an all-out riot on the streets of New York in 1903, involving the Eastmans, the Five Points gang, more than 500 cops, and an Irish gang called the Gophers, who had heard gunfire and joined the fray. The Gophers didn't choose a side; they just wanted to get in on the action. The battle ended only when all sides ran out of bullets.

In an effort to quell the mob violence, the Democratic political machine actually made Eastman and the head of the Five Points gang, Paul Kelly (born Paolo Vaccarelli), publicly shake hands and agree to "kiss and make up." When that didn't work, the police talked the two gang leaders into settling their dispute one-on-one in a fistfight, which they agreed to, but both parties claimed victory in the brawl.

Eastman was convicted of assault and sent to jail for ten years in 1904. In a strange turn of events, he was released from prison in 1914, enlisted in the army under the alias William Delaney, and served with valor during World War I. He was hailed as the poster boy of "rehabilitated" ex-convicts. That is highly debatable, however. What is indisputable is that a Prohibition agent shot him five times outside a Manhattan speakeasy in 1920. Given his war record, Eastman had a military funeral and more than 4,000 mourners paid their respects.

Il Duce versus the dons

Benito Mussolini was the fascist dictator of Italy from 1922 until his assassination in 1945, during World War II. It is to be expected that a totalitarian dictator and an organized crime family would not get along together. Like rivals in a Wild West town, the island of Sicily was not big enough for both of them.

During one of Mussolini's many parades, this one through a

Sicilian town, the local don, who felt the dictator was unworthy of respect, ordered the townspeople not to come out to line the parade route in tribute. To add to this flagrant disrespect, he had several bedraggled homeless men amble into the town square to hear the dictator's bombastic and bellicose ranting. This was just one example of the disdain that the Mafia had for politicians. As a result, the bullet-headed Mussolini went ballistic and launched a crackdown on the Mafia. When he was done, many Mafiosi had been tortured and killed, and most of the major dons were put behind bars. Ultimately, however, the Mafia would have the last laugh, with a little help from Uncle Sam.

Mussolini did not have a chance to fully rid Sicily of the Mafia. His alliance with Adolf Hitler and Nazi Germany launched Italy into World War II. Fueled by the desire to get rid of Mussolini, the Americans sided with the Mafia. Sicilian Mafiosi spied for the Americans during the Allied invasion of Sicily, and after the Americans kicked the Germans off the island, they allowed the Mafiosi to come into positions of authority.

Calogero Vizzini is one hoodlum who benefited from this Allied assistance—the Allies made him the mayor of his community. He and other Mafia men were given political offices because they were known in the communities and clearly commanded respect. Actually, it was fear more than respect. The citizenry knew the newly appointed leaders well as Mafiosi and would not dare oppose them. Vizzini ultimately became the "Boss of Bosses" of the Sicilian Mafia. In fact, the whole

Mafia made out like Sicilian bandits during the post–World War II era. Mafiosi became more powerful than ever and solidified their stranglehold on the island.

When Vizzini died in 1954, the Mafia experienced a metamorphosis. Gone were even the slightest pretensions of Old-World civility and honor. The younger generation were called "gangsters," a common and generic term in America. In Sicily, however, the dignified, albeit deadly Mafia of old disdained this low-class criminal element and its coarse manners and tactics. However, the Mafia of the 1950s descended to this level of "gangsterism." The Sicilians were even more bloodthirsty than the Americans when it came to their business practices. For one thing, they committed more murders, including the brazen assassinations of judges, police, and politicians, than did their American counterparts. The Sicilians were also more intertwined with the political sphere than the American Mafia. Business, politics, and even the Catholic Church interacted seamlessly in Sicily, working together to achieve their goals. With the exception of the occasional crusading reformer, the Sicilians accepted the Mafia as one aspect of its culture and the worlds of light and shadow did business with one another. Perhaps America is not as different as we would like to think.

The Mafia's appeal is due in large part to its larger-than-life cast of characters. For every weasel and rat, there were also plenty of giants. Twisted and evil giants, but impressive leaders and bold men of action nevertheless. It is a shame that these men didn't channel their often formidable skills into more positive pursuits. Instead, they chose a life of crime that, with some notable exceptions, proved true the old adage "Those who live by the sword will die by the sword."

From Al "Scarface" Capone to the "Dapper Don" John Gotti, this section will introduce you to some men whose names you may know, but about whom you

Part 2

People

will learn a few things that you probably did not know. You will also find out about a few figures whose names may not have become household words, but whose influence in making the Mafia the thriving enterprise it was for many decades cannot be underestimated. As you'll soon see, sometimes the least-known Mafiosi are the most lethal—truly cagey Mafiosi thrive in the shadows and disdain the spotlight.

Who were the Mustache Petes?

In Mafia lingo, the term Mustache Pete has nothing to do with facial hair and everything to do with attitude. It was an old slang expression for a conservative and cautious fellow, and this is what the young tyros who sought to seize power from the old guard called the earliest Mafia dons. These younger Mafiosi believed that the old boys were too traditional and Old World to make the Mafia a viable enterprise in the New World. The older regime was accustomed to tending their olives and tomatoes, or leisurely sipping a cappuccino or some vintage vino, while business got done at a leisurely clip. These guys operated on one speed only, and it wasn't fast forward. In contrast, the younger mobsters were lean and hungry, and such men are dangerous.

Joe The Boss Masseria and Salvatore Maranzano were the most powerful and influential of the Mustache Petes. Salvatore Maranzano originally studied for the priesthood in his native Sicily, but by the time he came to the United States in 1918, the Dark Side had seduced him. But Maranzano was not inclined to think outside the criminal box, and that made him a target for the up-and-coming generation of increasingly Americanized gangsters.

Maranzano's number-one nemesis among the "mainlanders" (gangsters with little or no ties to the Sicilian Mafia) was Joe The Boss Masseria. During the 1920s, Joe The Boss was New York's answer to Al Capone. He left his native Sicily with a price on his head, first seeing Lady Liberty in New York Harbor in 1903.

The Mustache Pete syndrome got its first kick in the pants when Masseria and a few loyal confederates attacked the Morello gang's headquarters and killed several loyalists. (The Morello gang was the current crop of hoodlum, whose forebears were the Black Hand in nineteenth-century New York City.) Masseria carried out additional hits until the hoods decided it was better to switch sides rather than fight. They consolidated under his leadership, and Masseria then became New York City's Boss of Bosses.

One of Masseria's protégés was the man who became known as "Lucky" Luciano. Luciano was not averse to mingling with the Jewish and Irish criminal element in New York City. Masseria, an insular Mustache Pete, did not approve—he wanted to keep things in the ethnic family.

Masseria remained, for the most part, unopposed until 1928, when Maranzano blew into town. The rivalry between the two Mafia dons would blow up into the first big mob war on American soil. There would be much "going to the mattresses" as the Mafiosi prepared for a long battle. ("Going to the mattresses" is a Mafia expression for preparing for and waging a long gangland war.) Mafiosi would literally leave their homes, head for a secret location, and live in military-style, barracks-like quarters, sleeping on mattresses on the floor in between shooting up the town. They would live in these conditions until the war was over. This particular bloody conflict began when Maranzano started hijacking Masseria's truckloads of bootleg moonshine and muscling in on his other various rackets. Known as the Castellemmarese War, the conflict was named for the town in Sicily that gave the United States so many Mafia hoodlums.

As the two Mustache Petes battled it out for supremacy in New York City, the real machinations were going on among the ambitious young hoods. These young upstarts were coming to the conclusion that they did not want to serve the winner of the war, no matter which one it might be. And the leader of the pack of wolves in waiting was a young Charlie Luciano, who would prove to be very "lucky" indeed. When the dust settled and the Tommy guns were silenced, the Mustache Petes were ousted and the modern Mafia was born. (See number 63 for more on how Lucky got this job done.)

Mr. Lucky meets his unlucky fate

Lucky Luciano might have enjoyed *The Sopranos*. Actually, a man of his generation would probably have preferred *The Godfather*, given its classier, epic, and Shakespearean nature.

Lucky Luciano made the Mafia a formidable force: He eradicated the Mustache Petes' narrow-minded Old-World thinking and created a modern criminal organization. He lived a long life and was one of the most ruthless and successful gangsters of the twentieth century.

Contrary to what some might believe, Luciano did not get his nickname from surviving the near-fatal beating that left him with a fashionable scar on his cheek, an emblem befitting his status as a tough guy. He was called Lucky because of his handicapping acumen. He could pick winners at the racetrack with uncanny accuracy. And most of the time the races weren't even fixed.

Lucky Luciano was a high-profile gangster. Unlike his lifelong pal, the low-key Meyer Lansky, Mr. Lucky was often seen at the trendiest nightclubs hobnobbing with the glitterati of the day. Living the high life took its toll on Luciano, though. Prostitution was one of his many rackets, and you could say he was a hands-on manager. In fact, he was so overly familiar with his staff that he developed multiple bouts of gonorrhea and syphilis. When the Mafia ventured into the drug business, Lucky Luciano made sure that he got most of the prostitutes hooked on heroin, in order to control them better. Luciano was doubly lucky in this case, as the prostitutes turned their profits right back to him to feed their addiction.

Indeed, Luciano was a bad man, but he was also colorful, and people have always been fascinated with a flamboyant villain. At the end of his life, Luciano sensed this. And like a greedy Mafioso, he wanted to capitalize on it, while feeding his ego in the process. Luciano's greed finally led him to try to make a few bucks selling his life story, something Mafia men of his generation would ordinarily never do.

From his exile in Italy (he was eventually deported by the U.S. government but continued to pull the strings from sunny Naples), he watched as an increasing number of Mafia-themed movies and television shows gained popularity. The original *Untouchables* show was a big hit in the early 1960s, and Luciano contacted a Hollywood screenwriter to discuss turning his life into a movie or television project. Maybe he figured that telling the story of his life was practically an inevitability, and he ought to be the one to "wet his beak" (grab a piece of the action) on the project first. Also, if he had a certain amount of input he could put his own "spin" on the saga and perhaps come off in a more sympathetic light than he deserved.

But the Fates had other plans. Luciano's luck ran out before he could see an "authorized" version of his life story hit the big or small screen. He died of a heart attack while waiting at the airport to meet his would-be Hollywood contact.

Celebrating diversity, Mafia-style

Al Capone, being American-born and exposed to many other ethnic groups while growing up, was not as clannish as other Mafiosi. He married an Irish girl and met his new best friend, Jake Guzik, in Chicago. Believe it or not, the guy was an Orthodox Jew and a family man. Even after Capone was jailed and spent his last years in a degenerative state in Florida, Guzik continued to be a powerful and revered Chicago mob figure. Capone's friendship with Guzik was part of the younger generation's willingness to mingle with men from other ethnic groups. The Old-World Sicilian Mafia did not deal with other crime outfits, and their lack of tolerance led to their decline and the rise of the Young Turks, who eventually became the venerable elder statesmen of the Americanized Mafia.

The Jewish Mafia men were not immune to the hypocrisy of their Italian buddies. In spite of being an Orthodox Jew, Jake Guzik was also a pimp. He and his brother Harry were procurers for the brothels of pre-Capone Chicago mobster Big Jim Colosimo. Colosimo's wife was also Chicago's most celebrated madam, Victoria Moresco. At the time, prostitution was the Chicago Mafia's big business. (This would, of course, change with the advent of Prohibition.)

Gangster Johnny Torrio (one of Al Capone's mentors) became Colosimo's right-hand man when he got to Chicago. Torrio was a stable gangster who did not indulge in the vices from which he profited. The same could not be said of Colosimo, who was spiraling out of control. A singer named Dale Winter wrapped Colosimo around her little finger, and the call of the siren distracted him from more important matters like survival. Torrio sent a low-level hit man by the name of Al Capone out to New York City to whack Big Jim. And this was Scarface's entrée into the Windy City.

Harry Guzik remained in the prostitution racket, but Jake rose within the ranks of the Chicago mob to become its chief accountant. He was instrumental in shifting the focus of business from prostitution to bootlegging. Perhaps the former was, on some level, distasteful to him. Perhaps the latter was simply more profitable after the advent of Prohibition. Whatever the overriding reason, the government's attempt to abolish alcohol was directly responsible for the rapid growth of the Mafia in the 1920s, as was the Mafia's growing willingness to work with gangsters of different ethnic backgrounds. The Mafia never became a Rainbow Coalition, but its minor adaptation to the "melting pot" contributed to its increasing power and influence.

15

Mafia, kosher style

In the 1920s and 1930s, there were quite a few Jewish gangsters who worked with the Italian Mafia. The Sergio Leone/Robert De Niro movie *Once Upon a Time in America* tells a fictionalized account of Jewish criminals who rose from immigrant poverty in Manhattan's Lower East Side during the early decades of the twentieth century.

The real-life Jewish Mafia included Meyer Lansky, Bugsy Siegel, Longy Zwillman, Moe Dalitz, and many others. They were the usual suspects in the typical array of Mafia crimes, including the ubiquitous murder and mayhem.

However, Jewish participation in the Mafia lasted only one generation. Unlike their Italian counterparts, Jewish gangsters discouraged their kids from going into the family business. In fact, Meyer Lansky sent one of his sons to the West Point military academy. In another interesting historical sidebar, the Jewish gangsters actually did some good when it came to fighting the Nazis in the years before and during World War II.

Before America entered the war on December 7, 1941, the isolationist movement in the United States was strong. While some of the isolationists simply did not want to get involved in someone else's war, a shameful number of Nazi sympathizers and anti-Semites were also rearing their ugly heads in America. Pro-Hitler rallies actually took place in New York City's Madison Square Garden and elsewhere, attended by men wearing their Nazi "brown shirts" and sporting the swastika, the Nazi's crooked symbol of hate.

Free speech is a cornerstone of the American experience, and anyone has a right to protest in a peaceful manner, but both law enforcement officials and the underworld were disgusted with these fascist love fests. In an unusual and very secret alliance, New York State Judge Nathan Perlman asked Meyer Lansky to have a few of his boys crash some of the rallies and dampen the enthusiasm by any means short of murder. Lansky, who was well aware of what was happening to Jewish people in Europe, happily obliged. Though a battle between the Mafia and the Nazis sounds like it might be akin to the matchup in the recent movie *Alien vs. Predator*, one cannot help but root for the Mafia in this one instance.

After World War II and the horrors of the Holocaust, Bugsy Siegel and other Jewish gangsters assisted the men and women fighting to establish the state of Israel with contributions of money and munitions. They were loyal to their own people, even if they were from different parts of the world. Of course, that doesn't mean that during their brief stint with the Mafia, they didn't wreak all sorts of havoc on people from lots of other ethnic backgrounds. After all, a bad man who does a good thing is still a bad man.

The Rat Pack–Mafia connection

Perhaps no other entertainer was more enamored with the Mafia and its brethren than Frank Sinatra. His association with the mob went all the way back to his early days as a saloon singer. From the 1930s through the 1970s, almost every crooner and comic had to deal with the Mafia, since the mob was involved in the clubs and other venues where they performed. In those days, most entertainers accepted this fact and got along with their employers. Sinatra, by all reports, had a schoolboy's romanticism when it came to gangsters. When he was down on his luck and his career was in a slump, it was his mob friends who still paid him to sing in their saloons. Sinatra was nothing if not loyal. When Las Vegas became one big Mafia-run party, he was there, and he brought his Hollywood sidekicks along with him for the ride. Together they created a slice of pop-culture lore that continues to fascinate people.

Sinatra's goombahs even gave him the option of purchasing 9 percent of the Sands Hotel, where he often performed. Old Blue Eyes always packed the house at the Sands, and all of those sold-out crowds of Sinatra fans inevitably wandered over to the casino's slot machines and gambling tables. Living the Las Vegas life was so good that Sinatra got it in his head to make a movie in Las Vegas. His idea ultimately became the 1960 film *Ocean's Eleven*, which is more memorable as a time capsule of an epoch than it is as a cinematic achievement.

Sinatra's Rat Pack pals included Dean Martin, Sammy Davis Jr., Peter Lawford, and Joey Bishop. Dean Martin, who was born Dino Crocetti, had Americanized his name, but his friends (and some fans) still called him Dino. Unlike Sinatra, this Italian-American crooner was nonchalant and did not fawn over his Mafia paymasters.

Peter Lawford, a singularly "unhip" addition to this randy band of aging bad boys, was there in large part because of his direct connection to the Kennedy family. He was married to Patricia Kennedy, JFK's sister.

The Rat Pack filmed *Ocean's Eleven* by day and performed at the Sands by night. Their show was called "The Summit," named for the Cold War conferences between the United States and the Soviet Union. Bishop largely scripted their endless stream of "ad-libs." In the grainy black and white snippets of the live show that survive, their hijinx seem juvenile and not particularly funny. Sammy Davis seems to ignore ethnic humor that would make even the politically incorrect of today a little uncomfortable. From the looks of the show clips, the audience loves it, however, and the performers seem to be having even more fun than the adoring throng.

In the midst of all of these antics stood the Mafia, smiling in the shadows. For every time Sinatra sang "Luck Be a Lady," lady luck no doubt ran out for countless hapless gamblers when they hit the casino tables later on; their losses continued to line the gangsters' pockets.

While the Rat Pack's performances helped greedy Mafiosi rake in the dough, it spurred some positive change as well. Up to this point in time, black performers were not allowed to stay in rooms at the Las Vegas hotels in which they worked. Despite performing for sold-out crowds and receiving standing ovations, they had to withdraw to a shantytown on the wrong side of the tracks at the end of the show. (Velvet-voiced crooner Nat King Cole was even instructed not to make direct eye contact with the swooning, fur-adorned, and bejeweled ladies in the audience.) But Old Blue Eyes helped to break the race barrier in Las Vegas. Sinatra made it clear that if Sammy could not sleep in a room and swim in the pool of the hotel, for which he was making plenty of money, he would no longer perform there. Thus, an ultimatum put an end to the discrimination against black performers in Las Vegas. But it wasn't a sudden spiritual transformation that prompted this change; pressure on the Mafia's purse strings was what really did the trick. Above all else, the Mafiosi had a shrewd sense of commerce and, in this instance, the color of money was what truly talked to their larcenous hearts.

Going Dutch

Dutch Schultz was born Arthur Simon Flegenheimer in 1902 to Jewish parents from the Bronx. He was something of a mama's boy and stayed close to his mother until his untimely demise. In a perverse way, he also remained true to his mother's deep faith.

Despite being a vicious killer, Schultz had a strong spiritual and metaphysical streak. Sometimes he would claim he was practicing Judaism; other times he considered himself Catholic. He was a gangster who gave a lot of thought to the afterlife. A man on a spiritual quest, he considered himself a religious hood.

But his so-called spiritual quest sure didn't impede his life of crime. He began his criminal career in the Bronx. Sent to prison at seventeen on a burglary conviction, he was a problem inmate and was transferred to a harsher prison. He promptly escaped, only to be recaptured. Committing the crime was a badge of honor among his Bronx buddies, who gave him the tough guy moniker "Dutch Schultz."

Like all Mafiosi, he was involved in the bootlegging racket during the 1920s. His area of expertise was beer, and he and his cronies controlled the beer distribution in the Bronx and Upper Manhattan. His gang was comprised mostly of Jewish and Irish hooligans.

Two of his associates went by the names "Fatty" Walsh and Edward "Fats" McCarthy. Obviously, these Irish lads were sampling the merchandise.

Crusading New York District Attorney Thomas Dewey had learned a lesson from the arrest and conviction of Chicago's Al Capone and sought to nail mobsters on income tax fraud. If it was good enough for Big Al, he figured, it might work with the New York Mafia, too. And so Schultz's bootlegging business came under scrutiny. While under indictment for tax fraud (it was estimated that he owed the IRS $92,000 and could face forty-three years in prison), Schultz went on the lam. He went "into hiding" for twenty-two months but never left New York City. Although the police could have picked Schultz up rather easily, if they had wanted to, he was seen in public often, continuing to take in the nightlife and other diversions that New York City had to offer, all in plain sight of the press, paparazzi, and the police force. Sure, he was in hiding, but given the corruption in the police force and among politicians, he did not have to vary his routine very much.

Eventually, however, Dutch turned himself in. He became a media darling during his two trials, the first ending in a hung jury and the second in an acquittal. While Luciano may have been lucky, Schultz proved to be very fortunate as well.

But not for long. The government indicted Schultz again, and he had had enough. He wanted to whack Dewey, which would have been a violation of the Mafia's rules against killing politicians. Murdering a prosecutor who was so squarely in the public eye would do much more harm than good. Dewey's wife had received threatening phone calls, and there was a $25,000 reward for his murder. The Commission (the Mafia's structure of hierarchy established by the Mustache Petes) would not sanction the hit on Dewey, but maverick Dutch boldly announced that he was going to "make it so" anyway. The truth is that his cronies fully expected him to go to jail on income tax evasion charges. In their mercenary minds, they were already imagining spending the money from Schultz's interests, which they planned to take over. They were more than a little disappointed when he beat the rap.

Albert Anastasia, alias "The Mad Hatter," a.k.a. "Lord High Executioner of Murder, Incorporated," confirmed Luciano's suspicions that Schultz was intent on assassinating Dewey. At that point, Luciano knew what he had to do. The Commission's decrees were final and not to be ignored. The price a Mafioso paid for ignoring them was the ultimate price.

On October 23, 1935, in the Palace Chop House in Newark, New Jersey, Dutch Schultz and three of his associates found themselves in a pitched gunfight with Murder, Incorporated. Schultz died in a nearby hospital days later. He converted to Catholicism on his deathbed, and his delirious dying ramblings are a legendary stream of consciousness mob-speak rant that inspired beatnik author William S. Burroughs to fashion a work called *The Last Words of Dutch Schultz: A Fiction in the Form of a Film Script.*

Hollywood hoodlum

While most hoods of his time kept a low profile, Benjamin "Bugsy" Siegel was one of the first of the celebrity gangsters. Tall, dark, and handsome, he became a darling of the Hollywood set, many of whom got a vicarious thrill flirting with danger. Starlets and other women who tended to fall for the "bad boy" type needed to look no further than this handsome psycho mobster murderer. No, Bugsy was not named after the wisecracking cartoon rabbit. He got his nickname because of his mercurial temperament and tendency to fly off into violent rages, which, in underworld parlance, was called "going bugs." Although he did not like being addressed by this nickname, he would prove its validity by pummeling the poor souls who had the nerve to call him "Bugsy" to his face.

Because of his violent antics in New York, his pal Meyer Lansky sent Bugsy out to California. There, he became fascinated with the glitter and glamour of Tinseltown and even had movie gangster and pal George Raft arrange a screen test. Believe it or not, the good-looking thug had aspirations to usurp Clark Gable and Cary Grant's popularity as a matinee idol.

Needless to say, you won't see Bugsy Siegel on the Turner Classic

Movies cable station, because he did not become a movie star. For whatever reason, his charisma did not translate to the big screen. Warren
Beatty, on the other hand, did do a very good job portraying the mobster
in a 1990 film called, appropriately, *Bugsy*.

Life might have been better, and certainly would have been longer,
for Bugsy Siegel had Hollywood welcomed him into its pantheon of
stars. His Hollywood ambitions never materialized, but moving West
did have its benefits for Bugsy. His legacy was in turning the small
desert town of Las Vegas, Nevada, into a Mafia pleasure palace and
moneymaking enterprise beyond the mob's wildly avaricious dreams.
Unfortunately, Bugsy was either guilty of mismanagement or outright
theft, because his monument to the Mafia, the Flamingo Hotel, took
forever to build and went way over budget. Bugsy's dream was to cre-
ate the ultimate gambling and entertainment complex, unlike anything
the world had ever seen. Meanwhile, back East the bosses were growing increasingly impatient, wondering why Bugsy's project was taking
so long. Even Bugsy's boyhood chum Meyer Lansky could no longer
cover for his uncontrollable pal. The mob was getting very angry, and
it is not wise to give a gangster *agita*.

One evening, Bugsy was alone in the posh Hollywood home of his
mistress Virginia Hill. She was a "bad girl" straight out of a B movie.
Bugsy was smitten with this failed starlet and career gangster's moll.
Many believe she was the one skimming the money from the mob,
and that Bugsy was blinded by love. (For more on Virginia Hill, see

number 60.) That night, at Hill's home, the air filled with the acrid scent of cordite as gunmen blasted Bugsy Siegel into "the big sleep." One of his baby blue eyes, which had once made many a starlet swoon, was found at the other end of the room.

The Mad Hatter

Despite his nickname, Albert Anastasia was nothing like the cute character from *Alice in Wonderland*. First a part of Joe Masseria's gang, in 1931 he joined up with Lucky Luciano and Bugsy Siegel, agreeing to get in on the scheme to knock Masseria off in a Coney Island restaurant. A key member of Murder, Incorporated, Albert Anastasia was one of the most vicious members of a vicious profession. Every man has his strengths and weaknesses, and Anastasia was more comfortable with the bloodlust aspect of the Mafia than the bottom-line business side. Although he was a killing machine, his "loose cannon" temperament led to his downfall.

After moving from Italy to the United States in 1919, Anastasia got his start on the Brooklyn docks, rising in the ranks of the mob-controlled longshoremen's union. A hot-tempered hood, he

killed another longshoreman early on in his career. The crime landed him a reserved room on death row, but he was granted a second
trial after four of the witnesses who had testified in the first trial
reversed their statements. When all four of those key witnesses suddenly went missing before the second trial could be held, Anastasia
walked. (This sort of thing has happened time and time again in the
history of the Mafia.)

In Anastasia's other trials over the years, witnesses had a tendency
to turn up dead, guaranteeing his acquittals. In one instance, a husband
and wife vanished, never to be heard from again. Though the blood
stains splattering their home were a clear indication of foul play, Anastasia still slipped off the hook. Another man was found in the trunk of
a car in the Bronx, and yet another was dumped in the Passaic River in
New Jersey.

Because of Anastasia's erratic personality, Lucky Luciano and
fellow mobster Frank Costello kept him on a reasonably short leash.
These cooler Mafia heads maintained a watchful eye on him. Anastasia
was loyal to these two bosses, but he remained unstable. And so with
Anastasia, the Mafia decided to implement its own version of the Peter
Principle, which holds that a person is promoted to the level of his com-
petence, and then is promoted to and remains at a level at which he is
*in*competent. Thus, Anastasia was promoted to the level of his incompetence. Anastasia was more interested in killing than making lucrative business deals. Though he was an accomplished killer, he was a

bad manager, and his lack of subtlety and finesse made him a liability rather than an asset in the long run.

Clearly, the Mafia didn't call Anastasia mad for nothing. Once, Anastasia even ordered the hit of a man he saw on television because the man had testified as a witness against celebrated bank robber Willie Sutton. (Sutton was the man who, when asked why he robbed banks, offered the now-famous reply, "That's where the money is.") Outraged at this witness's attitude, Anastasia had him murdered. Of course, this crazy whack job violated the mob's unwritten rule about not messing with outsiders. The fact that a high-level Mafioso would so casually order the hit of a "civilian" raised some serious red flags for the other members of the Commission. Despite the potentially serious ramifications, Anastasia remained nonchalant about the whole thing. His offhanded explanation was, simply, "I hate stoolies."

The mob dispatched Anastasia with a finality that the typical corporate "Peter Principle" person does not suffer. He did not have what it took to be a Mafia don, but he was not merely demoted or fired. Anastasia did not have the luxury of collecting unemployment insurance while networking with a few headhunters. Instead, some headhunters took care of him in one of the more notorious mob hits that will discussed a little later in this book.

Kiss me, Guido

Joe Valachi was the first Mafia informant to receive national media attention. Daytime television covered his testimony, but the events that transpired to land Valachi on the witness stand were enough of a soap opera in and of themselves to rival the likes of *The Sopranos*.

Joe Valachi became a member of Mustache Pete Salvatore Maranzano's organized crime family in the 1920s. He was officially "made" in 1930 and served at the pleasure of Maranzano until the don's murder in 1931. After that, Valachi was a soldier in the Luciano family, reporting to its head, Vito Genovese.

Valachi was an unrepentant hoodlum. He was a numbers runner, leg breaker, ruthless murderer, and, in later years, a drug trafficker until he was finally locked up. He went to prison on a fifteen- to twenty-year sentence for a drug charge when he decided to re-evaluate the oath of silence he took when he was "made."

Joe Valachi was in a federal prison in Atlanta, Georgia, and he found himself sharing a cell with none other than his old boss, Vito Genovese. Genovese became head of the Luciano crime family after Lucky Luciano was deported back to Italy, and the family eventually assumed his name. Things grew tense for the cellmates when Genovese began to suspect Valachi of turning traitor. At the time, Valachi hadn't even considered ratting anybody out, but Vito Genovese still gave Joe Valachi the "kiss of death," meaning that he was now a marked man. Even in prison, the Mafia could conduct business and have men killed. Valachi knew he would soon be whacked.

There were three attempts on Valachi's life while behind bars. When Valachi got wind of who the hit man might be, he killed him. But it turned out Valachi had killed the wrong man. His sentence was amended from fifteen to twenty years to life imprisonment. It was then that Valachi fulfilled Vito Genovese's prophecy and become an informant.

After he spilled the beans, Valachi was placed under witness protection and guarded by 200 United States marshals. They were not going to let the Mafia get their hands on their prize songbird. Not easily thwarted, the mob offered a $100,000 reward for Valachi's head on a platter. When Valachi appeared before the McClellan Commission in 1963, his testimony received national and international attention. (See number 98 for more on the McClellan Commission.) He fingered 317 organized crime members and brought the name *La Cosa Nostra* into the vernacular. The testimony was enlightening, but it produced no quantifiable results. Not one Mafioso was jailed based solely on Valachi's testimony.

The problem was that Valachi had no entrée into the inner workings of the Commission. He could only speak of his own experiences. Nevertheless, the lawmakers in Washington and the public were treated to a worm's eye view of the Mafia's workings. There was probably much braggadocio in his testimony and plenty of unreliable hearsay. Still, his pronouncements painted the picture of a brutal, nasty, and ruthless world: following strict codes of honor while double-crossing and backstabbing; going to church on Sunday and then beating a man to death on Monday; keeping girlfriends on the side once their wives became pregnant.

Enraged, the Mafia orchestrated something akin to a publicity campaign against Valachi's testimony. The Mafia even used Valachi's nickname to attack his character. He had been called "Joe Cargo" as a young man, but over time Mafiosi began calling him "Joe Cago." According to mob sources, they were not simply mispronouncing his moniker—*cago* is an Italian word for excrement.

At least Valachi exacted revenge on his former boss. Vito Genovese lost much of his power as a result of Valachi's testimony, and the crime family he controlled lost its pre-eminence as the largest and most powerful of the five families in New York.

Joe Valachi was released from prison and died of cancer in 1971. It is surprising that none of his former associates found him and whacked him. And, as if all the media attention he received during the trial wasn't enough, Valachi shared his story with the public once again before his death. He cooperated with bestselling author Peter Maas on the book *The Valachi Papers*, and Charles Bronson subsequently played him in the movie.

Analyzing Costello

Long before the movies *Analyze This* and *Analyze That* and television's *The Sopranos*, which portrayed Mafiosi who seek counseling as commonplace, mobster Frank Costello was the patient of a psychiatrist. Indeed, there is plenty to analyze when it comes to this unique and complex character. When Lucky Luciano was sent to prison in 1936, his henchman Frank Costello took over. Costello was a different breed of don. He was not a micromanager, nor was he into the sensational aspects of being a gangster.

He was more like the quiet Meyer Lansky, who pulled strings and made bundles of money but stayed out of the headlines. Costello was a "big picture" guy who looked beyond New York City to expand his family's interests as far west as Las Vegas and as far south as Cuba. Costello was affectionately called "Prime Minister" because of his diplomatic skills, and his ability to delegate leadership made his family a lot of dough.

Vito Genovese had served as Luciano's underboss, and by all rights he should have succeeded Mr. Lucky as boss. Genovese, however, left the country to avoid a murder charge and was languishing in Italy, and Costello stepped in. After World War II, Genovese came back to America, where he was expected to stand trial for the murder, but as often happens in Mafia murder trials, key witnesses were themselves mysteriously murdered. As a result, Genovese remained a free man, and he and Frank Costello vied for control of the Luciano crime family for many years. Genovese chipped away at Costello's power with a series of small but significant moves. A series of hits eliminated many of the top guns in Costello's corner. Costello countered by talking the hotheaded Albert Anastasia of Murder, Incorporated, into killing his bosses, the Mangano brothers, to keep the balance of power in his favor for a few more years. In 1957 Genovese orchestrated the barbershop murder of Albert Anastasia and staged an unsuccessful hit on Costello. Costello was shot and wounded in the lobby of his luxury apartment building on Manhattan's Central Park West. The hit man who missed was allegedly Vincent "The Chin" Gigante, who became one of the Mafia's most colorful characters. (See number 25 for more on Gigante.)

Carlo Gambino, an associate of Anastasia, actually helped Genovese with the Anastasia hit. Gambino then assumed control of Anastasia's outfit, and from thereon it was known as the Gambino family. True to form, Gambino quickly switched sides once again and joined an alliance with Costello and Meyer Lansky to take out the ambitious Genovese. (Once a backstabber, always a backstabber . . .)

Frank Costello wanted to get out while the getting was good so that he could enjoy his retirement. The Commission agreed to let Costello leave the underworld quietly. He enjoyed a comfortable and peaceful retirement and died in 1973.

King of the Hill

Another infamous rat in the history of Mafia informants is Henry Hill. Actor Ray Liotta played him in one of the best and most realistic gangster movies, Martin Scorsese's *Goodfellas*. And, in a very appropriate twist for these very twisted times, Hill became the first Mafia informant to have his very own Web site.

When Hill was a small boy on the mean streets of Brooklyn, he became enthralled with watching the local wiseguys. Like many a hoodlum before him, including Big Al Capone, Hill got his start running errands for the neighborhood gangsters, much to the chagrin of his parents.

Eventually, Hill became entrenched in the seductive criminal underworld. One of his best friends was Jimmy "the Gent" Burke, another local gangster who, alas, would never be "made." Hill and Burke were not full-blooded Italian. Because of this, no matter how many people they killed, they would never be admitted into the Mafia's inner sanctum. For the record, Hill says he never killed anyone, though he was present at a few murders.

Hill was a member of the Lucchese Mafia family, one of New York City's big five. His greatest score was the Lufthansa airport heist, for which his cut was a mere $50,000 out of a cool $5.8 million. Hill felt he was entitled to a lot more. His life was also spiraling out of control. Drug and alcohol addiction and its attendant paranoia, plus the increasing stress of living in the dangerous underworld, brought him to the breaking point. In 1980, he turned on his goodfellas and became, in their eyes, a very bad boy.

Most of the men that Henry Hill fingered, including Jimmy the Gent, were sent to prison. Burke died there. Dozens more were murdered as they squabbled over the distribution of the airport heist money. (See number 76.) Hill went into the Witness Protection Program and was given a new identity. He remained in the program for seven years.

But just because he started over with a new identity, that doesn't mean he went clean. Hill continued to engage in criminal activity and even did sixty days in jail. He was arrested for drug dealing, assault, burglary, driving while intoxicated, and parole violation. The protection program, run by the United States Department of Justice, kicked him out, so he turned to the FBI, which has helped him remain in hiding ever since.

Henry Hill now calls himself a "cyberfella." He is the author of a cookbook called *The Wiseguy Cookbook: My Favorite Recipes As a Goodfella to Cooking on the Run*, and he put out another book, *Gangsters and Goodfellas* (as told to Gus Russo), in June 2004. He even appeared on the Howard Stern show a few days before his book's release. Although his life will always be in danger, it would seem that his ego has compelled him to make potentially hazardous forays into the light.

Hill also has a Web site called *www.goodfellahenry.com*. It is a strange mix of gallows humor, showmanship, and salesmanship. Visit the site and you can buy copies of Mafia-related books and chuckle over Hill's version of a David Letterman Top Ten List, which lists Mafia slang expressions for murder. You can take an interactive tour of his old neighborhood and the mob hangout called Robert's Lounge. You can even buy an autographed poster of the movie *Goodfellas*, which he suggests you purchase before he gets whacked. Send Hill an e-mail and he might even answer.

These days, Henry Hill is clean and sober and wants to forge a new career as a substance abuse counselor. He is also trying to sell some movie scripts to Hollywood and a half-hour mob comedy television pilot. Needless to say, his favorite TV show is *The Sopranos*.

Pride goeth before a fall . . .

John Gotti, the last of the flamboyant celebrity Mafia dons, was undone in large part by his titanic ego and false sense of indestructibility.

Gotti was born into a poor family from the Bronx in 1940. His family moved to Brooklyn when he was a boy, and the angry young kid found himself in the land of the wiseguys. They became his heroes. Like Henry Hill and Al Capone, Gotti began his life in crime running errands for the local mobsters as a teenager.

He quickly became the member of a criminal street gang involved in car theft, robbery, and other criminal activity. He was arrested five times while still a teenager, but avoided any jail time, a bit of luck that would follow him through most of his career.

Gotti hooked up with the Gambino crime family when he joined a group of low-level hoods that reported to Aniello Dellacroce, who hung out at the Bergin Hunt and Fish Club, a storefront in a neighborhood of Queens called Ozone Park. Gotti's beat was near John F. Kennedy International Airport. The pack of thieves hijacked stuff that landed at the airport and had yet to make it to its final destination. If you have ever been told that the electronics or cigarettes you purchased "fell off the back of a truck," this means it was intercepted before it reached the merchant who bought and paid for it, and was sold by the Mafia at a discount to the consumer and a big profit to the mob.

Gotti rose within the ranks and ultimately seized power through a hit on Big Paulie Castellano, discussed elsewhere in this book, in number 69.

Most mobsters prefer the shadows, and those who strut and swagger in the limelight have invariably gotten their comeuppance. During the 1980s, many modest low-level capos (literally "captain" in Italian, meaning a Mafioso who supervises the soldiers) and underlings were ordered to meet with Gotti at his social club, even though everyone knew that it was under constant FBI surveillance. Camera-shy hoods were obliged to have their picture taken, lest they earn the wrath of Don John. It was common knowledge that the FBI saw and heard everything that was said in the club, but Gotti would make his minions line up and pay homage anyway. He would also speak with self-destructive candor. Membership in the Gambino family dropped considerably.

On a lighter note, the FBI's wiretaps of John Gotti also revealed his marital woes. "That woman is driving me crazy," he was heard to say about his wife and their tumultuous marriage. Keep in mind, when wiretaps are made public during Mafia trials, they are, of course, abridged and contain only conversations that pertain to the case. We hear about the crimes and murders both planned and committed, but the mike is on 24/7, so the FBI and other long arms of the law are treated to a veritable soap opera of family squabbles, discussions about what's for dinner, and all the other little day-in-the-life elements that even the most murderous Mafioso has in common with the average American family man. And, depending on where the microphones are strategically placed, the listeners are also treated to a variety of nonverbal sound effects that are emitted in the course of everyday affairs. Dedicated agents must endure thousands of hours of innocuous chatter and the sounds of various bodily functions while awaiting the incriminating statements that can place a criminal where he belongs—behind bars.

Bayou Boss

The New Orleans mob was always very independent. It went its own way and did not answer to the Commission up north, which regulated just about every other Mafia family, large and small. Just as the American South is regarded as being more laid back than the North, with people and events moving along at a leisurely pace, so too the New Orleans Mafia's structure was a looser confederation of individuals and groups of criminals.

Carlos Marcello, who stood only five-feet-four-inches tall, was a feisty little guy indeed. Made in the New Orleans Mafia by the age of twenty-five, Marcello is not as well known a name as Al Capone or John Gotti. And yet, he surpassed both of them in longevity and success. Marcello's spheres of influence included most of the Southern and Western states, including California, plus pre-Castro Cuba, the Caribbean, and Mexico. His illegal income funded numerous and diverse legitimate businesses.

   Both the Kefauver Committee and later the McClellan Commission went after him. Two prominent members of the Kefauver Committee were the Kennedy brothers, John and Robert, who would continue to harass the Mafia into the older brother's presidency. And perhaps they paid an awful price for their meddling.

   No doubt Marcello was well aware that their father, Joe Kennedy, made his fortune in the bootlegging business during Prohibition. He didn't think that these preppie pipsqueaks could do him much harm. Then again, he hadn't anticipated that one of them would become president and make the other the attorney general. Despite harassment from the Kennedy brothers, Marcello pleaded the Fifth over and over again and made no attempt to hide his contempt of them.

   There are myriad conspiracy theories about the assassination of JFK, and some place the blame squarely on the Mafia's doorstep. Many mention the Mafia as a player in a vast, dark scheme worthy of *The X-Files*. The facts relating to the Mafia are disturbing. Lee Harvey Oswald's uncle, a man named Dutz Murret, was a bookie for the New Orleans Mafia. Oswald's mother was also linked to several soldiers in the mob. The man who killed Oswald, Jack Ruby, had ties to the Dallas crime family, which was more or less a subsidiary of the Marcello organization. Is it possible that the Mafia used the oddball Oswald for their hit, and then had him whacked to avoid discovery? Future generations will know when the classified files are revealed. Carlos Marcello was in a New Orleans courtroom being found "not guilty" of his false birth certificate charges on the afternoon of President Kennedy's murder.

In an interesting coincidence, Marcello was also in court being acquitted of another charge on the afternoon that Robert F. Kennedy was assassinated in 1968. Some conspiracy buffs try to link Marcello not only to RFK's murder, but also to the killing of Martin Luther King Jr., in the same year. Though the "lone gunman" explanation is also questionable in both of these murders, the strongest circumstantial evidence links the mob boss with the JFK assassination.

After the Kennedy and King assassinations, Carlos Marcello and the New Orleans mob continued to prosper and avoid the long arm of the law for many years. But nothing lasts forever, and eventually the FBI caught up with him. In a yearlong surveillance operation, the feds accumulated hundreds of hours of damning recordings that captured Marcello mouthing off on a variety of topics, including his criminal activities. His office had been tapped, and many turncoats had worn wires in his presence. In 1981, after decades of seeming invulnerability, the don of the New Orleans Mafia was found guilty of violating the RICO law. (See number 90 for more on the RICO law.) He was also convicted on other charges in other states, and by the time all of the prosecutors compared notes, Marcello, at the age of seventy-two, had racked up a sentence of seventeen years in prison.

During the six years he was incarcerated, Marcello bounced around several federal prisons, most of them minimum-security "country club" institutions until he developed Alzheimer's disease and was released from prison. The mighty little man who once ruled a massive criminal empire, killed many men, and ordered the killings of many more (possibly even a United States president) degenerated into dementia and infantilism and died in 1993.

The Oddfather

In 1957, Vito Genovese orchestrated both the successful barbershop murder of Albert Anastasia and the unsuccessful hit on Frank Costello. Costello was shot and wounded in the lobby of his luxury apartment building on Manhattan's Central Park West. Vincent "The Chin" Gigante was the alleged hit man who missed. Gigante went on to become one of the Mafia's most colorful characters.

Gigante went from being a low-level gangster who couldn't shoot straight to a Don who (supposedly) couldn't think straight. The Chin had a unique way of keeping the law off his case. And it almost worked. Gigante was often seen wandering around his neighborhood in the Greenwich Village section of Manhattan wearing a bathrobe, talking to himself, and even urinating in the street. On account of this behavior, wags started calling him "The Oddfather." Few thought he was actually crazy; it was generally believed that Gigante was faking it, in an effort to avoid prosecution for his many crimes by copping an insanity plea. Although his dutiful family and his "family" maintained he was genuinely nuts, the feds were not convinced.

Unlike the hubris-laden Gotti, Gigante was keenly aware that the authorities might be listening in on his conversations. He rarely used the telephone and would not let underlings speak his name aloud. He would turn on the water full force and talk near the faucet in order to thwart any wiretaps. His people referred to him with a stroke of the chin (hence his nickname) and with gender-bending aliases that included Frank, Fitz, and Aunt Julia. But some dumbfellas would slip and accidentally refer to their dear auntie as "he." This was, of course, a giveaway to the eavesdroppers. Like the bizarre antics of many other Mafiosi, this would all be quite hilarious if it didn't involve so much murder and mayhem. Gigante finally went to trial in 1997 and was found guilty of racketeering and ordering the murders of two Mafiosi. He was acquitted in seven other counts of murder, but the convictions were enough to send the then sixty-nine-year-old to jail for twelve years, where he still resides as of this writing.

During the trial, Gigante never dropped his stumblebum routine. He was wheeled in and out of the court and usually stared vacantly at nothing in particular, sometimes muttering to himself. Several Mafia informants, including the king of the rats, Sammy "The Bull" Gravano (see number 35), testified that he was a big faker, and the jury believed them. The defense attorney naturally protested that the informants were saying what the government told them to say in order to get leniency.

For an alleged loony bird, Gigante managed to stay out of jail (and stay alive) for forty years, while running one of the most powerful crime families in America. Not bad at all considering so many "sane" Mafiosi ended up in cement galoshes, sleeping with the fishes.

Gigante is scheduled to be released from prison in 2007, assuming he is still with us. It makes you wonder: Will he don his terrycloth wardrobe once again, and resume his strolls up and down the sidewalks of New York?

Nitti Gritty

True enough, the conduct of real life Mafia men is often more melodramatic than their fictional counterparts. But there are times when a gangster's reputation and legacy are enhanced, however inaccurately, by Hollywood. Frank Nitti, a lieutenant of Al Capone, had a more memorable life on TV and in the movies than he ever did in reality. By all accounts he was not particularly impressive as gangsters go, and his end was nothing if not ignominious. The portrait pop culture paints of Frank Nitti is a different story altogether, and the real Nitti would no doubt have been surprised if he could have seen the way he was treated in movies and on television.

When Al Capone was arrested in Philadelphia for carrying a concealed weapon and did time behind bars, he left the business in the hands of his brother Ralph and his henchman Frank Nitti. After Capone was sent away for good, Nitti took over. Prohibition ended a couple of years later, but the Mafia had other rackets in its repertoire.

Despite his real-life duties, this Capone mob lieutenant was given more credit than he deserved when his character became a regular on the 1950s television version of *The Untouchables* and then a thoroughly despicable villain in the 1987 movie version. Neither version is accurate. The East Coast Commission did not respect Nitti, and he did not wield power as a criminal mastermind. But since Robert Stack's Eliot Ness had to have a formidable nemesis, veteran actor Neville Brand portrayed Nitti as a mob menace during the run of the hit show.

In the 1987 Brian De Palma movie version of *The Untouchables*, a thoroughly hissable Billy Drago plays Frank Nitti. However viscerally appealing it might have been, the real Eliot Ness did not throw the historic Frank Nitti off of the courthouse roof, as depicted in the movie.

In fact, Nitti committed suicide to avoid a stretch in the slammer. He didn't even live to see his fictitious namesakes become dastardly screen villains.

The cheapfather

When the Castellemmarese War ended, Joe Profaci took over one of the five New York crime families, and that family bore his name during his lifetime. Profaci had a bigtime reputation as a cheapskate Mafioso. He charged members of his family the equivalent of union dues. Each soldier and capo had to fork over $25 a month for the privilege of being in the family. And he always made sure that he wet his beak. The soldiers were told that these dues were to cover any legal fees they might incur during their criminal activities. They were also told the dues served as the equivalent of a "widows and orphans" fund. But the men in his organization never saw a dime of it returned to them, even when they needed it. And, unlike other unions, the members of the Profaci family were killed for nonpayment of dues. All this while Profaci lived the high life on a lavish estate. As a result, his men disliked him and his fellow dons did not think highly of him. Yet, he remained in the job until his death from natural causes in 1962.

But Profaci's unpopularity did prompt a mutiny in his ranks. Three brothers—Joey, Larry, and Albert Gallo—and others who were dissatisfied with Profaci's reign made plans to oust him. This saga came to be known as the "Gallo Wars." Profaci used the old "divide and conquer" technique employed by the ancient Romans (with whom the Mafiosi liked to compare themselves). He pitted one family against the other and thus thwarted a hostile takeover of his own family. The war ended when Profaci died of cancer.

Ironically, in spite of all the maiming, killing, and double-crossing they do, Mafiosi sometimes give generously to charities and go through the motions of being good, pious Catholics. Perhaps they are trying to assuage their guilt, or maybe they think they can buy their way into heaven. Like plenty of other Mafiosi before and after him, Profaci was also a devout Catholic. He even tried to get a Vatican knighthood, much as Michael Corleone did in the opening scenes of *Godfather III*. Profaci's bid was less successful. Law enforcement officials in New York let the Pope know what kind of a fellow he was, and that was the end of that.

Going Bananas

Joe Bonanno, a.k.a. Joe Bananas, ascended to power when Salvatore Maranzano, one of the Mustache Petes, was killed in 1931. This portentous event marked the culmination of the Castellemmarese War, which rid the streets of the Mustache Petes and established a new underworld order. The twenty-six-year-old Bonanno, hand-picked by Lucky Luciano himself, was the youngest man ever to head a family.

It was a small family, but Bonanno ran a tight ship. His was a presence that commanded respect. He was a natural leader of men, a Mafioso who could probably have put his people skills to good use, had he been inclined toward the straight and narrow.

Bonanno formed alliances with more powerful dons and made his family's fortune through gambling, loan sharking, and eventually, as all Mafia families did, drugs. But uneasy is the head that wears the crown, as the fella said, and in the 1960s the aging Bonanno believed that there was a conspiracy among the other crime family leaders to kill him, even suspecting his own cousin to be among the conspirators. Bonanno planned to hit all of his enemies in one fell swoop and become the boss of bosses. This action quite possibly inspired *Godfather* author Mario Puzo when he had Michael Corleone kill the dons of the five families in one afternoon.

The fictional Michael Corleone was successful. In Bonanno's version, however, one of the hit men assigned to the task, Joe Colombo, switched allegiances and spilled the beans to the opposition. The Commission summoned Bonanno to appear, but he refused and went into hiding.

Though Mafia crime families are usually called by the name of their founder or current don, they are not like royal families, where the heir automatically assumes the throne. This has only happened occasionally. Joe Bonanno had wanted his son to succeed him, but most within the family were not too impressed with this princeling. The Commission countermanded Bonanno's wishes and appointed a hood named Gaspar DiGregorio as new head of the family. Bonanno was kidnapped, and he vanished. It is believed to have been a staged kidnapping. He was poised to appear before a grand jury, so it is possible that it may have been a setup to avoid the heat. Joe Bonanno emerged from his mysterious disappearance after nineteen months, but he declined to say where he had been. Some believe he had been a prisoner of the Commission. It is thought likely that he was set free on the condition he would leave the crime scene quietly and permanently. He did no such thing. The Banana War, as the local news media liked to call it, was on. The Commission had replaced Gaspar DiGregorio with a hood named Paul Sciacca after DiGregorio botched a hit on young Bill Bonanno and his boys. Sciacca's team was no match for the Bonannos. Nevertheless, the war went on for years during the 1960s. It was an extended trip "to the mattresses," as the Mafia calls a protracted gangland war. Bonanno, who was by this time getting on in years, suffered a heart attack and headed for Arizona and retirement. The Banana War ground to a halt, and Sciacca took control of Bonanno's Brooklyn rackets.

Joe Bonanno lived to the ripe old age of ninety-seven. Before he died, however, he did something no Mafia boss would have ever considered in the old days. He wrote his memoirs and even agreed to let Mike

Wallace interview him on *60 Minutes*. In his thick Italian accent, he told Wallace that Al Capone was "a jolly fellow," and he defended his memoir by saying that "nobody can tell the story of Joe Bonanno but Joe Bonanno." Of course, Joe Bonanno, like most autobiographers, told the story of his life the way that he wanted you to hear it. For example, he always denied he was in the drug trade, yet the Bonanno family did a brisk business in the narcotics industry.

Like his father, who went public with his life story, Bill Bonanno was also not shy about revealing family details in print. Bill consulted with author Gay Talese on the book about his family, *Honor Thy Father*, and he has also been interviewed for a segment on *A&E Biography* about his famous father. This sort of conduct would have been unheard of in the old days and would probably have resulted in the media-hungry mobster being soundly whacked. Nevertheless, Bill Bonanno is still alive and kicking—at least for now.

Close, but no Cigar

Carmine Galante was a Mafia hit man who spent most of his adult life behind bars. Although he was able to muscle his way into power, he lacked the business acumen to keep it. He was nicknamed "The Cigar" because of his fondness for the noxious weed.

Galante's rise and fall is just one more example of the ruthless violence that has long been a trademark of organized crime. While working as an underboss for the notorious mobster Joseph Bonanno, Galante steered the Bonanno family into narcotics. He built their heroin trafficking operations and later expanded them from New York into Montreal, Canada. As a result of his successful operations, Galante eventually became Joe Bonanno's successor and attempted to gain control of territory dominated by other American crime bosses. His lust for power and control of profits generated by narcotics, pornography, loansharking, and labor racketeering ultimately led to his, some believed quite timely, demise. Galante was driven by a thirst for notoriety and profit, and his intentions to expand his operations resulted in his public murder in Brooklyn, New York, in July 1979.

Galante was tough and fearless and more than a little sadistic. He was also universally unpopular with the mobsters from all five families. The Commission had wanted Bonanno out of power so they could better control the unruly family, but in Carmine Galante they had a far looser cannon. The hit on Galante in 1979 came as a unanimous decision from all the members of the Commission both in New York and across the country. This psycho hood known as "The Cigar" lived and died with a stogie in his mug. When he was whacked in Joe and Mary's Italian Restaurant in Brooklyn, the cigar never even fell out of his mouth.

Crazy Joe

Joey Gallo, alias Crazy Joe Gallo, was a hood in the Gambino family. He got his nickname because he was a loose cannon and a hit man who really loved his job.

Early in his career, he and two of his brothers tried to overthrow notorious cheapskate mob boss Joe Profaci in what came to be known as the Gallo Wars. These Gallo brothers were the antithesis of the benign California vintners Ernest and Julio Gallo (the men who would "sell no wine before its time"). But in spite of their determination, the Gallos did not win the war. It seems they could whack no don before his time—Joe Profaci died of natural causes in 1962.

Toward the end of his criminal career, Gallo also tried to usurp Joe Colombo, from the crime family of the same name, and this proved to be his undoing.

Gallo was one of the few gangsters to develop a rapport and a working relationship with the African-American crime gangs in New York. He saw them as a growing force to be reckoned with, and decided to work with them in their common interests rather than engage in a battle royal for control of the streets. Apparently, even gangsters can celebrate diversity.

Actor Jerry Orbach, now famous for playing a cop on *Law & Order*, was a good buddy of Crazy Joe. Before television fame, Orbach was a New York stage actor, who ironically played a character called "El Gallo" in *The Fantastiks*, during which he was the first to sing the often-recorded syrupy standard "Try to Remember (The Kind of September)." Gallo was married in Orbach's Manhattan home, and Orbach was with Gallo on the night he was murdered. They were dining at Umberto's Clam House in New York's Little Italy after just having seen the infamous insult comic Don Rickles perform at a Manhattan nightclub. Members of the Colombo crime family interrupted what would be Crazy Joe's last meal and whacked him in retaliation for a hit on one of their guys. At least Crazy Joe had a few laughs on his last night on earth.

Gallo achieved posthumous recognition for the song "Joey," co-written by Bob Dylan and Jacques Levy, and the 1974 movie *Crazy Joe*, where he was portrayed by former Irish Christian Brother and the future *Everybody Loves Raymond* actor Peter Boyle.

Mad Dog versus Killer

While the Italian Mafia is notorious for its nefarious acts, all ethnic groups have their criminal organizations, and the Irish are no exception.

The most successful and ruthless of the New York Irish gangsters in the 1930s was a tough mug called Owney "Killer" Madden. He was a dapper dude who partied in the high society of the day. He had interests in the bootleg racket and was the owner of the Cotton Club, the legendary Harlem nightclub. (In fact, the diminutive Bob Hoskins played Madden in the Francis Ford Coppola movie called *The Cotton Club*.) Lucky Luciano treated Madden with respect, and they did business amicably.

Not so amicable was Madden's relationship with fellow Irishman Vincent "Mad Dog" Coll. Mad Dog was the epitome of the loose-cannon thug. He killed his first man when he was only nineteen, and in the course of his criminal career, he broke all of the Mafia's rules and codes. He worked for Dutch Schultz but eventually bristled in the role of second banana and started his own gang. In an attempted hit on Schultz that became a blazing gun battle, Mad Dog was responsible for causing something the Mafia tried to avoid at all costs. An innocent civilian was killed and four others were wounded. And not just any civilian. The victim was a five-year-old boy. This prompted unwanted media attention and public outcry directed at the Mafia. Mad Dog was about to be put out of his misery.

Mad Dog wanted to muscle in on Killer Madden's turf, and with names like those you know the battle could only end one way. Owney Madden won the bout, courtesy of Dutch Schultz. Mad Dog met a fate befitting his nickname: He was gunned down by Schultz's boys while making a call from a telephone booth on West 23rd Street in Manhattan. Reportedly, the only attendee at his funeral was his widow. Apparently she was loyal to that dog, rabid though he was.

Killer Madden fared better. He did a year in the slammer and then retired to Hot Springs, Arkansas. This was a Mafia resort town discovered by Al Capone, and it is famed for its natural and restorative mineral baths. Gangsters put it on the map, and ordinary citizens still flock there to "take the waters" and gamble at the world-famous racetrack, Oaklawn Park.

Diamond Man

Legs Diamond was perhaps the most shot Mafioso in history. Shot but not killed, that is. The Mafia's history is strewn with bullet-riddled bodies, but between 1919 and 1931, Diamond's body withstood having no less than seventeen bullets pumped into it.

Legs Diamond was part of a gang called the Hudson Dusters, which roamed New York City before World War I. He served some time in jail as a draft dodger from 1918 to 1919 and resumed his activities with the gang after his imprisonment. Around that time, Diamond took on a hit job for a hood named Little Augie Orgen. Actually, Diamond contracted the hit to a third party, but he got the credit. As a result, Legs became a well-known and successful bootlegger working for Little Augie and Arnold Rothstein, the man most famous for his alleged role in fixing the 1919 World Series.

In the late 1920s, Legs took his first bullet during an unsuccessful attempt to save his boss. Little Augie was in conflict with gangster Louis Lepke over control of the New York City Garment District. Lepke ordered a hit, and Augie and Legs were shot on a city sidewalk. Augie died; Legs took two shots and prudently made an alliance with Lepke.

Legs then came into conflict with Dutch Schultz over the bootleg business. Legs controlled Lower Manhattan; Schultz had Harlem, Upper Manhattan, and the Bronx, and he was eager to expand his business into Legs's turf. Attempting to avoid Schultz's hot squads, Legs hid out in various undisclosed New York City locations. Schultz's henchmen trekked all the way to Denver, Colorado, and fired more than 100 shots into the car of Diamond's brother Eddie. Amazingly, Eddie Diamond survived—and the hit men still could not find Legs. They finally caught up to him in upstate New York, in a hotel room with one of his many paramours. This time, they shot Legs five times. He spent some time in the hospital, but once again, he did not die.

In 1931, Legs moved permanently to upstate New York. There, he was the victim of a drive-by shooting. He was shot three more times and survived yet again. Two innocent bystanders caught in the crossfire were not so lucky.

Nobody's luck lasts forever, however. A final hit occurred at a girl-friend's apartment. That night, Legs had been out drinking, and he passed out on the bed. Finally, he was an easy target. The hit team fired two shots into his head. As they were leaving, one of the killers went back to fire one more shot into Legs's brain, just to make sure. This time, the Mafiosi got their man.

The Canadian godfather

We all know about Al Capone, John Gotti, and the fictional Vito Cor-leone, but how many people know Vito Rizzuto? No, he's not a rela-tion of Yankee "Scooter" Phil Rizzuto. He has, more infamously, been called "the godfather of the Italian Mafia in Montreal" by Canadian authorities. Just as many Italian immigrants came to the United States, others went to Canada. And the unsavory among them brought the Mafia along for the ride.

Rizzuto was born in Sicily in 1946, and his family emigrated to Canada in the 1950s. The Rizzuto family arrived in Canada with anything but a clean slate. Vito's father had served five years in a Venezuelan prison for cocaine dealing, and his mother was arrested in Switzerland and questioned about her role in a money-laundering scheme—she was released without being charged. Rizzuto has been compared to John Gotti in that he is Canada's version of a Teflon Don. The Canadian authorities have gone after him many times but have thus far been unable to make any of their charges stick. To the embarrassment of prosecutors and the Royal Canadian Mounted Police, Rizzuto was acquitted of drug trafficking charges in 1986 and 1989.

His only serious conviction came in 1972, when he was found guilty of intent to commit arson. Of course, Rizzuto claims to be nothing more than a legitimate businessman. Canadian prosecutors claim otherwise. He is alleged to be associated with the Sicilian Mafia and, curiously, the Hell's Angels. He has also been linked to Canadian gangsters Maurice "Mom" Boucher and Joe LoPresti. (LoPresti, who was connected to the Gambino crime family, was murdered in 1992.)

In spite of his other, more heinous offenses, Rizzuto, like Capone, got nabbed over tax charges. In 2001, his impending trial was abruptly canceled when an out-of-court settlement was reached. Rizzuto's lawyer stated that his client wanted to avoid what would surely be a media circus. Also, most of the government's case would be a laundry list of accusations about Rizzuto's alleged ties to organized crime. According to Rizzuto's attorney, although these charges were of course false, his client would be branded a gangster in the court of public opinion and his reputation would be forever ruined. So, Rizzuto, guilty or not, agreed to pay all his back taxes plus hefty interests and penalties to avoid staining his community standing. (If only the prosecutors in the Capone case had offered him the same chance . . . No doubt Big Al would have jumped at it.)

Of course, a man is innocent until proven guilty, but there is much circumstantial evidence to make the case that Mr. Rizzuto may very well be the Canadian Godfather, indeed.

Self-proclaimed love god

Born Giuseppe Antonio Doto in 1913, this Mafioso changed his name to Joe Adonis after coming to America. He stowed away on a cruise ship at the age of thirteen and lived on the streets of Brooklyn, committing petty crimes during his first years in the New World. He was arguably the most sexist Mafioso, and that is saying a lot. The Mafia has never been a politically correct establishment, and its track record regarding women's rights would hardly endear them to the National Organization for Women.

Adonis's name suited him. He was a vain man who found himself irresistible and naturally assumed no women could resist his charms either, yet his first stretch in jail was for rape. Upon release, he joined the crime family of Frankie Yale, Al Capone's mentor. He also became pals with Lucky Luciano. In fact, during the elimination of the Mustache Petes, Adonis was one of the hit men who whacked the Mustache Pete leader Joe Masseria, the hit that put Luciano in power and began the Commission, which, in turn, gave rise to the modern Mafia. Throw in the other three hit men—Albert Anastasia, Bugsy Siegel, and Vito Genovese—and you've got a veritable who's who of gangland.

Although Adonis was placed in charge of Lower Manhattan, he ran things from an innocuous sounding base of operations, Joe's Italian Kitchen in Brooklyn. He dabbled in all sorts of business, both legal and illegal. After buying hundreds of cigarette machines, he then instructed his men to hijack cigarette delivery trucks en route to the New York area. Then he stocked his machines with the stolen cigarettes. At that point, virtually everyone who bought a pack of smokes from a vending machine in New York was filling Adonis's coffers.

In spite of these schemes, Adonis kept a low profile and was never the target of any criminal investigations. After Lucky Luciano was imprisoned and later deported to Italy, Adonis became a major player in the Commission. Though not as well known as many of his Mafia contemporaries, he wielded enormous power and influence behind the scenes. While exiled, Luciano visited Cuba to meet with fellow Mafiosi and reclaimed his authority in 1948. Adonis took it in stride and relocated to New Jersey. He had enough money to keep him happy and to indulge his many vices.

Adonis's free ride came to a halt when he was called before the Kefauver Committee and pleaded the Fifth on every question. (For more on the Kefauver Committee, see number 94.) Since he never bothered to become an American citizen, he was easily deported. Back in Italy, he enjoyed a pleasant retirement until one day, in 1972, the Italian police took him from his home for what proved to be a rough interrogation. No longer a young man, he died of a heart attack during the aggressive question-and-answer session.

John Gotti's Judas: Sammy "The Bull" Gravano

John Gotti took some serious gambles conducting Mafia business, even as he was being wiretapped by the FBI. Longtime second banana Sammy "The Bull" Gravano and others were alarmed and angered by the Dapper Don's egotism and big mouth. He had begun, as many celebrities do, to believe in the publicity hype, that he was the "Teflon Don," to the point that he considered himself as "untouchable" as Eliot Ness.

Sammy was born in Brooklyn, New York, in 1945 and fell into a life of crime at an early age. Sammy developed a violent temper as a youngster, perhaps in part because he was dyslexic. Dyslexia was not understood or treated back in the day, and Sammy suffered the slings and arrows of childhood humiliation, which, in turn, fueled his rage and antisocial tendencies. Perhaps if dyslexia had been diagnosed and treated back then, Sammy would have turned out to be a model citizen. On second thought, probably not.

Problems for Gravano arose when Gotti got wind of yet another impending indictment—one that would probably charge him with the murder of Paul Castellano. Gotti ordered Gravano to go into hiding since he knew Gravano would be subpoenaed to testify. Sammy the Bull stayed in various resort areas: the Poconos, Florida, and Atlantic

City. When he retuned to New York City, Gotti demanded that Gravano meet him at the social club everyone knew was wired better than a home entertainment center. They were not there fifteen minutes before the feds raided the joint.

As a result, Sammy the Bull went on to become the most infamous of the Mafia informants. His testimony destroyed Gotti's empire and turned the Teflon Don into the Velcro Don. Many mobsters believed that, while the Bull's testimony was certainly damning, the Dapper Don did himself in through his own hubris.

Sammy confessed to murdering nineteen people over a twenty-year period, an average of about one whack per year. His testimony not only brought down Gotti, it also toppled several other members of the Gambino family, as well as members of the Colombo and Genovese crime families. The Bull was granted immunity and entered the Witness Protection Program.

While in the program, Sammy did not behave himself. Living in Arizona with a new identity, he was arrested and convicted for being the brains behind the state's largest Ecstasy ring. And he made his drug business a family affair. Not only was his wife in on it, so were his son, daughter, and son-in-law. Ironically, back in his days as a murderous Mafioso, he was against the mob's growing involvement in the narcotics trade. Apparently he had a change of heart along with his change of name, address, and social security number.

Girl gone wild

Women who have a penchant for the "bad boys" should learn a lesson from the life and death of a woman named Janice Drake. Hers is not a famous name in Mafia legend, but her story serves as a cautionary tale. A bad boy can do more than break your heart; some bad boys will get you killed.

The name Anthony Carfano is also not as famous as Lucky Luciano or Frank Costello, but he was a contemporary and associate of these men. Carfano was not as dapper a don as John Gotti, but he sure was a snappy dresser. He was not as good-looking as Joe Adonis, but he was also a ladies' man. He controlled New York City's Garment District, along with Louis Lepke, and he was charged with murder six times over the years but never convicted.

Carfano was whacked in a parked car in Queens in the late 1950s. He was not alone. There was a woman with him at the time, and she wound up with a bullet hole in her forehead. Her name was Janice Drake.

The police assumed she was a gangster's girlfriend who was in the proverbial wrong place at the wrong time. But this was not the typical Mafia modus operandi. Mafiosi usually kept the "civilians," as they called them, out of their internal squabbles. Vito Genovese had ordered a hit on Carfano, so his fate was more or less a done deal. Barring going under deep cover and staying there, begging the feds for protection, or having sheer dumb luck, if a Mafia don wanted you hit it was a safe bet that your days were numbered.

But why Janice Drake? A little delving determined that Janice Drake was much more than an innocent bystander.

Janice Drake was the wife of a comedian named Alan Drake. Yet she did not deny herself the company of other men, mostly men of a criminal bent. And she was, by coincidence or otherwise, the last pair of blue eyes more than one Mafiosi beheld. She was with Albert Anastasia the night before he was whacked in a barbershop, and she was also with a shady garment-district denizen named Nat Nelson on the night of his demise.

The Queens district attorney determined that Janice Drake was a bagman, or bag woman in this instance, for the Mafia. (A bag person is someone, often outside the Mafia, who physically delivers ill-gotten loot from one locale to another at the behest of the mob. Some do it for a small fee, others do it to pay off a debt or curry favor, and some do it for the thrill.) Janice Drake did not need the money. She apparently got a kick out of rubbing elbows, and other body parts, with gangsters. And it proved to be a fatal attraction, indeed.

The DeCavalcantes: The real-life Sopranos

The DeCavalcantes of New Jersey are the basis for *The Sopranos*—at least that's what they like to think. Since that fictional crime family is New Jersey-based, the DeCavalcantes naturally assume the show is all about them.

For more than seventy years, this crime family controlled all the construction unions in the state, boasting that no hammer was nailed within New Jersey state lines without a kickback going to them. They were involved in auto dealerships, hotels, and restaurants. They had a hand in every mall that popped up in suburbia during the 1970s and '80s. They even controlled several Wall Street brokerage firms in the 1990s.

Most of the original family members hailed from the same town in Sicily. And they had an Old-World mindset as well. They eschewed the limelight unlike many of their more flamboyant counterparts across the Hudson River. The five families thought of them as second class, but, until the end of the line, the DeCavalcantes had fewer prosecutions and convictions than their more ostentatious New York neighbors.

The DeCavalcantes were also like their Sicilian forebears in that, when push came to shove and their backs were against the wall, they ordered hits on public officials and prosecutors, and dealt with traitors and informants by not only killing them, but by wiping out their entire family.

In the 1990s, the government cracked down on the family; many members, in turn, cracked under pressure and broke their vow of omerta. The ones who turned rat were from Brooklyn and Staten Island. No member of the family who lived in New Jersey, and no one who was born in Sicily, cooperated with the feds.

More than seventy-five members of the family were jailed between 1999 and 2001. All the leaders, including every capo save one, were prosecuted and imprisoned. The DeCavalcantes were beheaded essentially, and the body of their organization has twitched and jerked in death throes ever since.

Among those brought down in the family's crash was the *consigliere*, Stefano "Steve the Truck Driver" Vitabile. Vitabile was also the former driver of the most infamous don of the family, Simone "Sam the Plumber" DeCavalcante. The consigliere for more than thirty years, he was sent to jail for a variety of racketeering and murder charges. Not a man known for celebrating diversity, he ordered the murder of one family underboss named Johnny Boy D'Amato. He was killed because the word got out that he was bisexual.

Once they knew their days were numbered, the family members planned to bring in a Sicilian hot squad to take out the judges, prosecutors, informants, and all their families. But the family heads were behind bars before the plan could be implemented.

As of this writing, almost all of the leaders of the DeCavalcante clan are either in jail or under the Witness Protection Program. The rest of them are hanging out in New Jersey watching *The Sopranos* on HBO and living vicariously through the images on their TV sets.

Mafia legend is hardly the stuff of King Arthur and the Knights of the Round Table, but it is compelling all the same. It captures the imagination of ordinary citizens and Mafia members themselves. Everyone loves a good story with interesting characters, life-and-death struggles, and a little sex and violence thrown in for good measure.

In the movie *The Man Who Shot Liberty Valance*, one of the characters confronts a journalist with the true story of what really happened during that famous titular shooting. But the journalist opts not to tell the truth and sticks with the often-told but inaccurate version. He says, "When the legend becomes fact, print the legend."

Part 3

Legend and Lore

In this section, you'll learn about some of the more famous and infamous entries in Mafia lore. Some are true, some are partially true, and some may be the stuff that mythology is made of. They involve a diverse cast of characters that include not only the most celebrated names in gangland, but also such strange bedfellows as Benito Mussolini and Frank Sinatra.

What's in a name?

As previously mentioned in Part 1, the American Mafia has its origins on the island of Sicily, off the coast of Italy in the Mediterranean Sea. Throughout much of Sicily's ancient history, the predominant criminal was the bandit. These bandits terrorized the Sicilian countryside and gave rise to the first crime families in Sicily. The organization of these crime families was, for the most part, fairly simple. One alpha male ruled the roost. The less macho members followed him, with the occasional up-and-coming bandit challenging and defeating the leader.

The goals of the bandit gangs were also rather simple: Raid any vulnerable town or village, and rape and pillage. There was no code to live by, no notion of honor. It was essential for the bandit leader to instill fear in the rest of the bandit gang. Through fear, the leader maintained control. Intimidation and threats of bodily harm and/or death were the ways that a bandit leader stayed in power. Meanwhile, the communities the bandits preyed upon lived in a constant state of terror.

Throughout history, Sicily has been occupied time and again by various foreign invaders. The French were in control of the island of Sicily when the Mafia, as we know it, came to be. It is natural for oppressed peoples to form secret societies, and in Sicily, the native men banded together in groups to discuss their situation and their plans to fight the oppressors. In all tyrannies, freedom of assembly is forbidden and punishable by imprisonment or worse. The oppressors know that, as the old saying goes, in unity there is strength, and therefore they cannot safely allow the oppressed to join together, for fear of losing power. Nevertheless, the oppressed population often *does* manage to come together in a covert and clandestine manner.

The native Sicilians who banded together to form secret societies battled pirates, bandits, and other assorted outlaws that plagued the peasants. But it was through fighting for the oppressed peoples of the island against a common enemy—the French—that these individuals gained their power.

Some of these men were brave and patriotic and became heroes of the people. According to legend, they became real-life Robin Hoods and Zorros, battling the French invaders and instilling a national pride in a conquered people. Beyond the story of the woman who cried out upon learning of her daughter's injury at the hands of a French soldier (see number 1), there are a few other theories about how the actual word *Mafia* entered the Italian and, later, the English languages. One such theory purports that *Mafia* began as an acronym for the rallying cry of the Sicilian resistance forces. *Morte alla Francia Italia anelia!* is translated as "Death to the French is Italy's cry!" As you can see, the first letter of each Italian word spells *Mafia*.

Another belief holds that *Mafia* is derived from an Arabic word meaning "refuge." This interpretation also makes sense because, during the course of Sicily's violent history, people regularly ran for the hills to seek refuge from the current invaders. You probably remember the opening scenes of *Godfather II*, with the young Vito Corleone in his native Sicily. It was a hilly, rocky terrain where the natives hid, planned, and took potshots at the invading forces. Whatever the origins of the word *Mafia* might be, over time it came to be used widely in Italy, and then in America.

Wild, Wild Midwest

For many years, Al Capone had a free ride in Chicago. The politicians and police were shamelessly corrupt. The people wanted their vices, and Capone was more than happy to provide them. Cries of outrage and calls for reform from the political machine were nothing more than lip service. Chicago was a wide-open town where the mob ruled. "Big Bill" Thompson, the mayor of Chicago from 1915 to 1923, is considered to be one of the most corrupt men in the pantheon of American politicians. And that's no small accomplishment.

Despite all of this lawlessness, real reform was slowly making inroads into the Windy City. A man named William E. Dever succeeded Thompson as mayor, and he promised to crack down on the vice and corruption in his town. The Mafia took Dever's ambitions in stride. One reformer at the top was only a minor inconvenience when the rest of the team was more than eager to play ball.

So the Capone outfit moved down the road apiece to the small town of Cicero, Illinois. They simply bought the town lock and stock with the smoking barrels of their machine guns, using bribery as needed. In short order, Capone controlled all the prostitution, gambling, and bootlegging in the town. He even took over the racetrack. Capone's brother Frank acted as liaison with the corrupt local government.

As this was going on, one maverick journalist named Robert St. John openly opposed Capone's invasion of his newspaper. Because of St. John's efforts, it looked like Capone's handpicked politicos might lose the election of 1924. Capone used muscle to try to sway the voting public. To ensure victory, his goons loomed around polling places, making it clear which candidate would be the "healthiest" choice. The cops were called in response, and Capone's brother, Frank, was gunned down. Allegedly, Frank pulled his revolver when he found himself surrounded. A dumb move, if indeed it's true. The law deemed that the police had acted in self-defense when they killed him. At the end of the day, Al Capone still owned Cicero, but at a terrible price—his brother's blood.

After this tragedy, Capone vented his frustration by shooting a small-time hood who had dared to direct an ethnic slur at the little big man. Capone went to trial for the first time in his life, but he beat the murder rap. Witnesses were hard to come by, as was always the case with Mafia trials. Even though he walked free, the highly public trial had consequences for Capone: It made him something most mobsters did not want to be—famous.

Few twenty-five-year olds achieve the power and wealth that Al Capone had at that young age. And few people have to deal with murderous rivals and regular assassination attempts. Such is the price you pay for being King of the Underworld. Capone knocked off opponents, and they, in turn, were out to get him. One attempt on his partner, Johnny Torrio, was almost successful. The volatile hoodlum Bugs Moran pumped several shots into Torrio as he was entering his apartment building, but Torrio survived. Capone stayed with him at the hospital, even sleeping on a cot at the bedside of his friend and mentor.

Torrio got out of the business after being shot; he decided to retire and move to Europe. He also turned over his share of the massive empire to Capone. Success spoiled Capone. He moved into the palatial Metropole Hotel and lived the very public life of a media darling and national celebrity. He was a showman gangster who attempted to cultivate a Robin Hood image. He was a regular Joe who provided a service that the public wanted, a man who was misunderstood and harassed by the authorities. Or so he wanted people to believe.

Bugs Moran had attempted to kill Capone's good friend Johnny Torrio, and Capone was not a man who forgot such things. Moran was still operating in Chicago, and Capone's plans for revenge culminated in the single most famous incident in the annals of Mafia lore.

In addition to almost whacking Torrio, Moran had twice tried to hit another Capone pal by the colorful name of "Machine Gun" McGurn. Capone ordered a hit on Moran as revenge. Since Capone was spending that winter at his lavish estate in Florida, he left the hit in McGurn's murderously capable hands. McGurn hired out-of-town talent and planned to lure Moran to a garage on the morning of February 14. The bait was a stash of quality booze at a good price. The hit team would be dressed as cops. Moran and company would think it was a raid, not an assassination. When the moment arrived, the phony cops burst into the garage, simulating a police bust, made the hoods line up against the wall, and then mowed them down. But there was good news and bad news: The good news was that the hit went off without a hitch. The bad news was that Bugs Moran did not show up that day. The target of the hit had a guardian angel—or perhaps Cupid—on his shoulder that Valentine's Day. Everyone knew who ordered the hit, but no one could prove it, since Capone had been in Florida. The murders captured the fascination of the nation and have become as mythical an event as the Gunfight at the OK Corral. In addition to the sensational media attention, the powers-that-be in Washington began to take a closer look at the shenanigans taking place in Chicago. President Herbert Hoover announced that he wanted to see Capone behind bars.

Al Capone was eventually convicted of income tax evasion and sent to prison for an eleven-year stretch.

Vendettas, old and new

American Mafiosi's credo that they "only kill their own," was not the mandate of the old Sicilian Mafia. The old regime resembled the South American drug cartels in its penchant for wiping out the entire families of their enemies. One particular code the Sicilian Mafia followed closely was the obligation to seek vengeance against anyone who attacked a member of the family. In its very insular unity, the Sicilian Mafia took an assault on one member of the family as an attack on the family as a whole. The Old-World term for this is vendetta. The Sicilians took this obligation to an extreme that the American Mafia did not. The Sicilians routinely and ruthlessly wiped out anyone and everyone, including the small children and babies of their enemies.

The modern Colombian drug cartels are also notorious for massacring entire families of their enemies in particularly nasty ways, including the murder of women and children. This would have horrified many of the older American Mafia dons, had they lived to see the horrors that drug traffic wrought on the innocent. In fact, Mafiosi took such pride in their rule about "only killing their own," that anyone who violated that rule would be killed. Albert Anastasia and Dutch Schultz, among others, paid the ultimate price for taking their violent impulses out into the community at large, rather than keeping things "in the family."

Did your mother ever admonish you that "what goes on in this house stays in this house"? So too the American Mafia never liked its dirty pinstriped suits aired in public.

The Commission

The Mustache Petes, the conservative Old-World dons who were wiped out in the Castellemmarese War (1928–1931) established the Commission. The Commission was made up of the dons of the five big New York families and the lesser families in cities across the country. After the Mustache Petes' demise, a new breed of Mafiosi, led by Lucky Luciano and Meyer Lansky, retained the basic structure of the Commission, sometimes calling it the National Syndicate.

The Commission was one of the most successful and long-running "corporate" enterprises in the history of American "business." For the

most part it ran smoothly. Decisions were made and disputes were settled with a minimum of hard feelings. And when it came time to whack
someone, a vote was taken. Hotheads who took it upon themselves to
knock someone off were often killed, especially if they targeted someone outside of the Mafia.

Today, law enforcement believes that the Commission is now a
shadow of its former self, just as the golden age of the Mafia is long
past. However, its heyday lasted longer and it accomplished much more
than many American companies that have risen and fallen over the
decades. The Commission slipped into decline not because its structure was unsound but because the successive generations of Mafiosi
became more ruthless and less artful in doing business. Despite the
regular bursts of violence throughout the Mafia's bloody history, the
founding fathers of the Commission were men of subtle finesse compared to those who followed.

As mentioned above, the Mustache Petes originally devised the
Commission, and when Lucky Luciano seized power, he retained the
basic rules of order. But Luciano restructured the group into the so-
called five families. At the head of every Mafia family, there is one
man who calls the shots: the *capo di tutti capi*, or the boss of all bosses.
He is called the *boss*, the *don*, or sometimes the *godfather*. He con-
fers with the heads of the other families during Commission meetings.
He has usually achieved his exalted state through violent means, often
through the murder of the position's previous occupant. Directly below

the boss is the aptly named *underboss*. He is the second most powerful member of the crime family. He deals with the day-to-day operations of the family and has a more hands-on approach than the don. He is also called *sottocapo*.

Third in this triumvirate is the *consigliere*, or counselor. (Think of Robert Duvall's character, Tom Hagen, in *The Godfather.*) This person is the chief adviser to the don in all matters of policy. He is often, but not always, a lawyer. These three heads of the family are also called *the Administration*. Like the top officers in any legitimate corporation, these are the people who make the decisions, though in the underworld, termination has more finality than a pink slip.

At the lower levels of the Mafia, there is the *caporegime*. He is the equivalent of a lieutenant in the crime family. Usually called *capo* for short, he controls a crew of about ten or so underlings. Capo is also the diminutive of *capodecina*, which literally means "captain of ten." These crews commit the crimes, report the results, and surrender the lion's share of the loot to the capo. The capodecina sees that the money flows upward to his masters.

Below the capos are the soldiers. They are also known as *sgarrista*. These are the grunts who get their hands dirty. These crews carry out the heists, hijackings, and hits that make up the day-to-day workings of a typical Mafia family. The soldiers are all "made" men, meaning they have been indoctrinated into the family, have taken the vow of omerta, and have committed at least one murder. Lower ranking soldiers are called *piciotto*. Lower soldiers are also made men, but they must continue to work hard and prove themselves in order to get promoted to the rank of *sgarrista*.

Next down on the Mafia food chain are the *associates*. They are not made guys. Although not actual members of a Mafia family, they work with the crews in their various nefarious acts; they are eager beavers who dream of being made. If they are not full-blooded Italians or Italian-Americans they can forget about it. As Jimmy Burke of the Lucchese family was well aware, Irish need not apply.

Another name for associates who warrant special respect is *Giovane D'Honore*. These are not made men, and they are usually non-Italians, but their contribution to the family business is appreciated. That sort of person is also called "connected," meaning that he is tight with the family without being an actual member.

Other key "white collar" gangsters include the *contabile*, or financial consultant, and the *chief corrupter*. The equivalent of a high-powered accountant, the contabile does not get his hands bloody. One thing is certain—this bean counter is sure to dot every *i*, cross every *t*. His masters would not tolerate accounting errors. The *chief corrupter* is the member of a crime family whose job it is to corrupt police, judges, elected officials, and others. The chief corrupter does not always appear in the hierarchical flow chart, however. A made man need not hold the position. The only requirement for this position is that it be held by someone with the means to influence the "legitimate" world.

Other denizens of a Mafia crime family include the many "crews" that engage in all manner of mischief, including heists and hijacking. They report directly to the capo. Many of these junior-league gangsters are called *cugines*. They are ambitious young hoods who desperately want to be made. Though valuable (they are more than willing to hit, whack, ice, or burn any target, since this is a prerequisite to being made), the elder gangsters often look upon them with wary eyes, since they may be a threat sometime down the line. These guys are also known as *Young Turks*.

A *chairman* is consultant or adviser to the Commission, or National Syndicate. A *district man* is a crime family officer whose turf covers a small section of a city or suburban area. He is also sometimes known as an *area man*. A *field man* is a mobster-manager who supervises a group of numbers runners, or Mafia errand boy. He is in charge of making sure the numbers runners visit regular customers, take the bets, collect the money, and return it to the "office."

An *enforcer* is a tough guy who uses violence to send a message from his Mafia superiors. He is also known as a *leg breaker*, *head crusher*, *muscle*, and a *goon*. An independent is a bookie who is not a Mafioso, but pays a tribute to be allowed to stay in business. He is kind of like a franchise operation. Lowest of the low is the *empty suit*. He is a Mafioso wannabe, a hanger on who is regarded with contempt by the members of the family.

42

How can I kill thee? Let me count the ways

There are many ways to kill a person in the Mafia handbook—and even more ways to describe it. Nowadays, because of the numerous Mafia movies that have been made and the television hit *The Sopranos*, the secret is out. The general populace and the FBI wiretappers are not fooled by these once-cryptic code words and phrases.

As we know, the Mafia uses murder as the ultimate hostile take-over. It is a part of the organization's business plan, a bullet point in its unwritten mission statement. But the Mafia does not kill with random bloodlust. The men in the Mafia who have done that have themselves been killed because of the problems their chaotic behavior caused. The Mafia practices due diligence, waiting until the headmasters give the order to kill an enemy. And when a person is killed it is usually done dispassionately, unless the target has done something particularly annoying to the dons.

A victim can meet his demise in any number of ways. He might be whacked, hit, iced, clipped, offed, burned, rubbed out, or popped. The hit man can *break an egg* or give his quarry a *serious headache*. The unfortunate fella could be fitted with *cement shoes*, a *cement jacket*, or put in a *cement coffin*. This type of murder is specifically for burials at sea, when the body, sometimes alive and sometimes not, is weighted for deposit in the deep blue, where the incriminating evidence will never be found. Such a victim is said to be, like Luca Brasi, *sleeping with the fishes.*

A don may order a hit in a variety of ways. With the approval of the Commission, he can put out a contract on the target of a hit. This makes the target individual *marked* for death. Another way to say it is to *put the X on* someone, as in *X marks the spot.* There's also a more intimate way to order a hit on someone—by publicly giving that person the *kiss of death.* This is a sure sign that his days are numbered. That person is now a *goner.* He is soon to be *put to sleep.*

Before a hit takes place, the hit man may have already been told to *get a place ready*, or to find a good location to dispose of the body. That means the target is *going*, as in "going, going, gone." The victim will then be *taken for a ride.* Or perhaps he'll go out for an *airing.*

Maybe he will get *five times thirty-eight*, which is five bullets in the head with a .38-caliber revolver, or maybe he'll be on the receiving end of a *Little Joe* if he failed to pay a gambling debt. A Little Joe is four shots in the head in two rows of two bullet holes. Neatness counts.

The unfortunate target of a hit could also receive the *Italian rope trick*, otherwise known as strangulation. Or maybe a *Sicilian necktie*, which means he'll be garroted with piano wire. An *ice pick kill* means what it sounds like—an ice pick through the ear and into the brain. One thing you never want to hear a Mafioso say is the word *buckwheats.* He is not referring to the beloved tyke from the *Little Rascals* and *Our*

Gang comedies. It is a slang expression for an especially grisly murder in which the victim is mutilated and tortured for an extended period of time before being put out of his misery.

On very rare occasions, the person may be given *a pass*, meaning his life is spared on account of the mercurial whim of the don. Lucky soul . . .

The gangster and the dictator

Mobster Bugsy Siegel had more than just a small bone to pick with the Italian dictator Mussolini. Siegel hated Mussolini on two counts—as a Mafioso and as a Jew. As such, Siegel concocted a crackpot plot to assassinate Italian dictator Mussolini personally. Not only had Mussolini jailed many Sicilian Mafiosi and adversely impacted business, he was also an ally of Adolf Hitler. Even before the concentration camps were liberated at the end of the war, there were stories about what was happening to European Jews under Hitler's tyranny. Hitler was quite outspoken about his Final Solution—his intent to commit genocide on the Jewish people. He wrote of it in his book *Mein Kampf* (My Struggle), published in 1925. At the time, Winston Churchill was one of the only voices in the wilderness warning the world about this madman. The rest of the world's leaders ignored the prominent red flags until it was almost too late.

Jewish gangsters did their part to thwart a burgeoning movement of Nazi sympathizers in America and helped the country in the war effort against the Germans. Make no mistake, though—they were not purely altruistic. Mobsters were always looking to "wet their beaks" in the process.

Siegel planned to ingratiate himself with members of the Italian aristocracy. When he was invited to Italy for an audience with Mussolini, he would then whack the dictator the good old American Mafia way. What is curious about this plan is that Siegel must have known that he would not get out of the room alive if he were to assassinate Mussolini on his own turf. But that didn't stop Siegel from talking about it, and the rational Meyer Lansky became deeply concerned whenever his friend would ramble on about this crazy scheme. Siegel wasn't nicknamed "Bugsy" for nothing. Given the hubris of most Mafia men, he probably felt indestructible and believed that he could pull off this insane scheme and make a clean getaway. Is it possible that this psycho killer was willing to make the ultimate sacrifice for noble motives—to rid the world of an evil dictator and save millions of lives in the process? We will never know. This would not be one of the many gangland hits Siegel orchestrated and participated in during his violent life and times.

Instead, of traveling east to Italy, Siegel headed west to Las Vegas, Nevada, where he got himself in trouble with his associates and paid the ultimate price for his fiscal irregularities. The world would have been a very different place if crazy Bugsy Siegel had been more motivated and encouraged in his plan to hit Mussolini.

Yale man

One of Al Capone's two Mafia mentors was a gangster called Frankie Yale (born Francesco Ioele). Yale owned a bar called, ironically, the Harvard Inn, where he hired the eighteen-year-old Capone as a bartender. In this gin mill Capone made the remark that changed his life.

Capone learned about business finesse from his first mentor, Johnny Torrio; Yale schooled him in the more brutal arts of the Mafia. Capone became proficient at both during the course of his notorious career.

Yale is believed to have killed twelve men before his twenty-first birthday. He and Johnny Torrio were partners in the Five Points gang of Brooklyn. When Torrio left for Chicago, Yale took over the New York territory. He sent Capone there a little later, when it got too hot for the pudgy scar-faced kid in Gotham.

Yale helped out his pals by dropping into Chicago for the occasional murder. His was an unknown face in the Windy City, so a victim would not be alarmed when he saw Yale coming. Yale whacked Torrio/Capone rivals Big Jim Colisimo in his nightclub (though other reports allege the shooter was Capone himself) and Irish mobster Dion O'Bannion in his flower shop. (It seems curious that a gangster would own a flower shop. At least he could send his victims flowers at cost.)

When Capone took over the Chicago mob, things between him and his former mentor became strained. Yale was responsible for the shipments of bootleg booze that landed on Long Island and worked their way to Chicago. More and more of these shipments were being hijacked en route, and Capone suspected Yale of a double cross. It turns out Yale was hijacking it himself, then selling it to Capone again, who was, in effect, paying for it twice. Capone sent a spy to check up on Yale and the spy was promptly whacked—but not before the informant confirmed Capone's suspicion.

Capone ordered a hit on Yale, who died in a hail of bullets on a street in Brooklyn. He was killed with a Thompson machine gun, the celebrated weapon of choice in Chicago. This was the first time the Tommy gun had been used in the Big Apple. The message was clear: The hit had come from Capone himself.

45

Birds of prey

There is a line in *The Godfather* spoken by Don Barzini, one of Don Corleone's rivals. Barzini wants Corleone to be generous and share his influence over the many politicians and judges he has on his payroll with the other Mafia families. Barzini tells Corleone he may present a bill for his services, adding, "After all, we are not communists."

In a twisted manner, the Mafia's leaders were participants in and advocates of the free enterprise system. Just like the CEOs of any big corporation, they were enthusiastic capitalists. The Mafia did not advocate the overthrow of the government and the American way of life. They were no threat to the status quo—in fact they thrived under it.

In the movie *The Godfather III*, a similar conference takes place decades later, when the older Michael Corleone wants to divest his family of all Mafia ties and, at long last, become legitimate. Michael gives the other Mafia dons generous payoffs and his thanks, but they are not satisfied. They want in on his new business. They want to use Corleone's international conglomerate as a vehicle to launder the money they've acquired in their criminal enterprises. Corleone will have none of it, but the dons are insistent. "We just want to wet our beaks a little," one of them says.

This phrase is a deceptively benign description of a common Mafia practice. It is an old Sicilian expression for taking a cut of the action in a certain business, whether you are invited to participate or not. Someone who does not want to share is said to "eat alone," and this is considered rude. What is not offered graciously will be taken by force.

Here's how it all works: Mafiosi traditionally approach a business and announce their desire to participate. In their minds, they don't want a lot. They aren't greedy men. They just want to wet their beaks a little. Usually what the Mafiosi offer in return is protection. Never mind that the aforementioned protection is, of course, protection from *them*. If the businessperson declines this generous offer, then the various forms of intimidation kick in. The harassment begins with verbal threats, and the intimidation escalates from there until the businessperson is made that famous offer that he cannot refuse. The Mafia started this tradition back in Sicily with the Black Hand, and Mafiosi brought it with them to America—and everywhere else in the Western World where they have a presence.

46

Strange bedfellows

John F. Kennedy had a presidential libido that was unrivaled until Bill Clinton came along. The difference is, back in that simpler time, the media didn't salivate over every scandal, and salacious gossip was reserved for the tabloid rags. And so the Washington press corps discreetly kept mum about the many stories of shenanigans circulating around the nation's capital. There was respect for the office of the presidency in those days. In fact, during the administration of Franklin Delano Roosevelt, most Americans did not know that he had been stricken by polio and was wheelchair bound, only able to stand with the aid of braces. Nowadays, with twenty-four-hour cable news networks and the ratings-hungry media, it would be impossible to keep such a secret.

One of JFK's many conquests was a party girl named Judy Campbell. Frank Sinatra had introduced them. Sinatra and his notorious Rat Pack were working hard for JFK's presidential campaign, and from 1959 to 1960, the senator from Massachusetts was spending a lot of time, sans his elegant wife Jackie, at Sinatra's mansion, where the middle-aged men indulged their bad-boy fantasies. Kennedy envied Sinatra's cool, and Sinatra envied Kennedy's patrician bearing and sense of "class." Sinatra, having come from humble beginnings, was obsessed with the notion of class. Yet, it would seem that the average working stiff struggling to put food on the table often exhibits more of this so-called class than the well-to-do Kennedy clan has during its long history of public service and private scandal.

Just to complicate this potentially explosive situation further, it turns out Old Blue Eyes had also introduced the alluring Ms. Campbell to Chicago Mafioso Sam Giancana. The president and the Mafia don essentially were "dating" the same woman at the same time. JFK and his brother had been actively involved with prosecuting organized crime, and would be even more aggressive when JFK became president and made RFK the attorney general. Politics makes strange bedfellows, indeed.

Kennedy and Giancana continued to consort with Ms. Campbell well after Kennedy was elected president in November of 1960, and FBI boss J. Edgar Hoover had evidence of this triangle live on audiotape. Hoover made the attorney general aware, and RFK, in turn, informed his brother. Hoover presented the information as if it was his goal to protect the president, but, of course, he was really putting the Kennedy boys on notice. The Kennedys were nothing if not political animals, so JFK, probably reluctantly, severed all ties with Sinatra, though not with the ladies.

You got some 'splainin' to do

Robert Stack played Eliot Ness in *The Untouchables* TV series, which first aired in October 1959 and ran until September 1963. After the 1987 movie became a big hit, Stack starred in the TV movie *The Return of Eliot Ness*. This was a purely fictional outing, and Stack was a little long in the tooth to play Ness, who died in his middle fifties.

The Untouchables was a violent program, a Tommy gun shoot-'em-up on the mean streets of 1930s Chicago. By today's standards it is rather tame, but it shocked many viewers in its initial network run. CBS received many complaints from parents who were concerned about the impact the show would have on their children.

Most of the protests, however, came from Italian-American groups. The old Cagney and Bogart mobster films rarely used Italian surnames for their characters, but *The Untouchables* made no secret of the ethnicity of its villains. Capone and his cronies were mentioned by name, and many took this as an ethnic slap in the face. In fact, among other people, Al Capone's widow even sued the producers! (The shows two-part pilot revolved around Ness's pursuit of Al Capone.)

Desilu Productions, the company run by the two classic TV icons Lucille Ball and Desi Arnaz, produced *The Untouchables*. At one point,

Desi received death threats from the Mafia (although it's not known which particular gangster made them), and he was thus obliged to travel with bodyguards. The ever-volatile Francis Albert Sinatra even accosted Arnaz in a Hollywood restaurant and chided him for his involvement in such a scandalous show. Desi, who was famous for telling Lucy she had some "'splainin'" to do, was now on the receiving end from Old Blue Eyes.

The mob was not pleased with its depiction in *The Untouchables*, but rather than resort to the old horse's head in the bed trick, Mafiosi hit the producers where it really hurts—in the wallet. (In the book and movie *The Godfather*, Don Corleone kills a movie producer's prize racehorse and leaves the head in his bed in order to intimidate him into giving someone a part in a movie.)

L&M cigarettes was one of the show's sponsors. Back in those days, tobacco advertising was allowed on TV, and many stars puffed away as paid spokespeople. Mobster "Tough Tony" Anastasia threatened to use his clout with the unions to make sure that millions of cartons of L&M cigarettes would sit on the loading docks, unpacked by the longshoremen and undelivered by the truckers, if L&M didn't drop its sponsorship of the show. L&M did so and in short order, costing the network and all those concerned a lot of money.

Not every hood was indignant about *The Untouchables*, however. As in any other corporate hierarchy, the CEOs resented the bad publicity, but many of the rank and file were delighted. Many low-level enforcers turned into wannabe screenwriters and actors. They contacted the producers with story ideas and even suggested that they would be "naturals" to play Ness's latest nemesis.

Nevertheless, because of all the flak, some compromises were eventually made to appease the viewing public. The earlier episodes had been presented in a documentary style, and the gangsters Ness battled were based on real people—hence the controversy and the lawsuits. When the real-life Ness nemeses were exhausted, the TV Ness took on other hoods the real Ness never even encountered, such as the malevolent matriarch Ma Barker. Producers also decided to throw in some fictional villains—who were prudently given non-Italian sounding surnames—to fight. Plus, in order to highlight an Italian-American good guy on the show, the actor who played Nick Rossi, one of Ness's team, got more lines.

Though the real Untouchables were long gone by World War II, the fictional Ness was still operating in Chicago in the 1940s and matching wits with Nazi saboteurs. *The Untouchables* ran for four seasons and has been in reruns ever since.

48

Murder, Incorporated

Just as any business will routinely contract the services of an exterminator, in the 1930s, the Commission decided it would be beneficial to have an elite corps of killers permanently on the payroll. These guns for hire were known collectively as Murder, Incorporated.

Lucky Luciano and Meyer Lansky were determined their business needed a security force. More than a security force, however, the mobsters developed a ruthless hit team that "rubbed out" the opposition, giving new and extreme meaning to the term "hostile takeover."

Murder, Incorporated, was an internal execution squad. It did not go after law enforcement officials, journalists, or politicians. As we shall see, a celebrated gangster was himself whacked when he became hell-bent on violating this code. The old saying that the Mafia "only kills its own" was attributed to Bugsy Siegel, a friend of both Luciano and Lansky.

Most of the members of Murder, Incorporated, were Jewish gangsters. These methodical hit men worked out of a Brooklyn candy store. They did not operate without orders, and, for the most part, their hits were well thought out and dispassionate. Hits required the unanimous approval of the Commission. Murder, Incorporated, operated nationally, so the hit men got to see America as they plied their trade. A simple shooting was the common form of execution, but staged accidents, faked suicides, and the occasional garroting were also accepted practices. Often, because the bodies were never found, law enforcement officials were forced to write the murders off as missing-person cases.

One of the two top members of Murder, Incorporated, was Louis Lepke, born Louis Buchalter. His early mob antics in the 1920s involved using threats, intimidation, and worse to break garment workers' union strikes. He also paired with Lucky Luciano in the bootlegging racket, and later became the main hit man for Murder, Incorporated, carrying out hundreds of hits. Lepke was eventually convicted on a narcotics charge, but while in jail some informants ratted him out, and so he was ultimately convicted on a murder rap. In 1944 Lepke and two other Murder, Incorporated, alumni, Mendy Weiss and Louis Capone (no relation to Al), met their maker at Sing Sing courtesy of Old Sparky (a slang expression for the electric chair). Lepke was the only high-ranking member of the Commission to suffer such a fate. The number-two man of Murder, Incorporated, Albert Anastasia, had been promoted long before Lepke's execution. (For more on Anastasia, see numbers 19 and 72.)

Most hits went unsolved, except for those revealed by the rats that squealed, and until Anastasia took power, they remained insular in their targets. If you had no business dealings with the Mafia, you were in no danger of getting whacked. No one will ever know for sure, but conservative estimates place the number of Murder, Incorporated, hits somewhere between 500 and 700 during its ten-year reign of terror. Murder, Incorporated, met its demise when several low-level members were arrested and began to "sing" to the authorities. The most famous was a man named Abe Reles, who was called the "Canary." He gave the police information on about 200 murders in which he was directly or indirectly involved. He was in police custody when he decided to "take a dive" out of a hotel window. Since it's unlikely that Reles took his own life out of guilt over turning traitor, it's generally assumed that he was given a gentle nudge. Although the end of Murder, Incorporated, didn't mean the end of Mafia violence, the days of an organized and efficient "Praetorian Guard" were over (the Praetorian Guard was a unit of bodyguards in ancient Rome who protected the Roman emperor).

Two wise guys in Wisconsin

When we think of the Mafia we tend to conjure images of Don Corleone and Tony Soprano, of blazing Tommy guns in gritty urban environs. Madison, Wisconsin, may seem like an improbable locale for a

Mafia family, but the FBI says one existed there, and its don was a man named Carlo Caputo. Caputo and his alleged Mafia family were like Bigfoot sightings. People swore it was out there, but it was not an "in your face" family like the boys in New York and Chicago.

The shadowy Caputo allegedly had ties to the Chicago and Milwaukee mobs, but less is known about him than his more famous associates. Caputo came to America as a sixteen-year-old in 1919 and made his way to Madison in 1940. Prior to this, he was purportedly a member of the Milwaukee Mafia family. In Madison, he lived in the Italian part of town, was successful in real estate, and opened restaurants, bars, and liquor stores. These were all seemingly legitimate enterprises, and to the unsuspecting residents of Madison, Caputo was merely a successful entrepreneur.

Caputo's only brush with the law was a thirty-day stretch for income tax evasion in 1961. Other than that, he continued to expand his seemingly above-board businesses. When an associate of Caputo's named Joseph Aiello died a natural death in 1970, the FBI probed into his affairs and determined that Aiello and Caputo were a two-man operation, boss and underboss of the smallest Mafia family in history. Caputo died at the age of ninety and went to his grave denying the government's charges. If he was in the Mafia, all crime families should be so low-key and nonviolent.

Madison's citizenry and political leaders lauded Caputo as a strong civic leader and for his role in the development of the city's business district. As a Mafia "kingpin," he ran his family for fifty-three years and died of natural causes. Not bad for a man in that line of work.

A horse is a horse . . .

The famous "horse's head" scene from *The Godfather* is believed to be based on an event from Frank Sinatra's life. For decades it has been assumed that the character of Johnny Fontane is based on Sinatra. That much is obvious. It is also well documented that Old Blue Eyes was great pals with many notorious Mafia men. However, it is unlikely and perhaps a little libelous to suggest that the revival of Sinatra's flagging career was prompted by the decapitation of a horse.

Frank Sinatra was at a low ebb in his career in the early 1950s. After initial success as a teen idol in the early 1940s, both he and his audience of swooning bobbysoxers had grown up. Sinatra's records were not selling very well and his movie career had been reduced to embarrassing epics like *The Kissing Bandit*. Added to this, he had suffered a throat hemorrhage that altered his voice from its reedy boyishness to a more macho-sounding tone. This, of course, would ultimately be a blessing, but he did not know it at the time.

Sinatra's claim to fame at the time was that he was married to the beautiful rising star Ava Gardner. Wagging tongues eager to kick Sinatra when he was down called him Mr. Gardner and Ava's Gardener. Sinatra felt humiliated.

Around this time, he became aware of the bestselling novel *From Here to Eternity* by James Jones. It was a brutal indictment of the peacetime United States Army in the days before the Japanese attack on Pearl Harbor on December 7, 1941. Sinatra recognized that the supporting role of Angelo Maggio, a skinny, doomed young soldier, was tailormade for his talents. Unfortunately, nobody else agreed with him.

Nevertheless, he lobbied aggressively for the role and eventually beat out method actor Eli Wallach. Just how Sinatra got the part has been the subject of much debate. Despite the rampant rumors of the Mafia using its muscle and menace on the Hollywood community, it is more likely that Ava Gardner used her considerable influence with dictatorial studio boss Harry Cohn to get Sinatra the part. Actually, what she got him was the opportunity to screen test for the role. Sinatra's talent landed him the part, and he won the Academy Award for Best Supporting Actor of 1953. At the same time, he signed on with a new record label, Capitol, and began collaborating with arranger Nelson Riddle. That collaboration revived his musical career and catapulted him back to the top, where he more or less remained for the rest of his life, until the lyrics of "My Way" became all too literal for Old Blue Eyes.

Conspiracy theory

In 1978, Congress's House Assassination Committee determined that there was a "probable conspiracy" in the death of JFK. The government has disavowed the "lone gunman" theory, though members of the committee maintained that Oswald was indeed the triggerman. Among the voluminous testimony given to the Warren Commission (the Congressional investigation that produced thousands of pages and is today regarded as unsatisfactory), much involved the Mafia. Santo Trafficante, a mobster active in the Cuban casinos, told a Cuban associate that he need not worry about Kennedy's re-election in 1964. The veiled threat is obvious.

The House Assassination Committee took great pains to pin the conspiracy on the Mafia. Oswald's mob connection and his assassination by a known mobster closed the case. There was a conspiracy, they admitted, but it was the Mafia and nothing but the Mafia.

It is a fact that the Mafia saw the island of Cuba as a cash cow and a personal pleasure paradise. Mafiosi had a nice deal going on. The military dictator Batista was their man, and they did business with impunity. Then Fidel Castro and his rebel forces took over the country and booted out Batista and the Mafia. The Mafia was miffed, to say the least. So was the United States government. It originally thought Castro would play ball with them, but he turned out to be a communist and allied himself with the former Soviet Union. It is worth noting that Castro is a ruthless, brutal dictator and not the noble rebel that, prior to more than forty years of tyranny, some Americans once regarded him as. (Even in more recent times, famous Americans have hobnobbed with the dictator. Steven Spielberg met with Castro and called it a "great experience." Jack Nicholson smoked Cuban cigars with him and declared the country a paradise. Their talents notwithstanding, these men prove that there are still plenty of people who are grossly out of touch when it comes to Castro, even though there are plenty of Cubans living in America today who could tell them a thing or two about Castro.)

It is also a fact that the CIA, exiled Cubans, and the Mafia were allied in a program called Operation Mongoose during the late 1950s and early 1960s. All these parties had a vested interest in ousting Castro by any means necessary.

In April of 1961, an army of Cuban exiles faced military disaster when they attempted to invade Cuba. That mission failed in large part because President Kennedy, at the last minute, denied them the promise of air cover from the Air Force. Many Cubans died on the beach during that attempt, and President Kennedy made a lot of enemies on that day. On November 22, 1963, it is likely that one or more of those enemies—perhaps a Castro supporter or one of those exiled—exacted revenge. (JFK had enemies on all sides of this conflict, including the communists, the anti-communists, the CIA, and the Mafia.)

As Joe Pesci, playing the frenetic David Ferrie in the movie *JFK* says, "It's a mystery wrapped in a riddle inside an enigma." Perhaps the mob was behind the assassination. Perhaps it played a small role in a larger scheme. Or perhaps there was a deeper, darker, more insidious conspiracy that used the Mafia as a patsy. Mafiosi, as powerful as they are, possibly could have been the fall guys for an even more sinister entity that makes the Mafia seem like penny-ante grifters in comparison. Perhaps our descendants will one day know the whole truth, when classified government documents are opened to the public, a process that has been happening gradually, although the last of the documents still won't be available for two decades.

Gilded cages

Lest you think a Mafia family's business ends when a don goes to prison, this isn't the case. Through the years, Mafia kingpins have often run their families and enjoyed fine dining and female companionship behind bars. Take what happened when Lucky Luciano was sent to the Clinton State Prison in upstate New York. This prison, also referred to as Dannemora, was not a model modern rehabilitation facility, nor was it considered to be as "comfortable" as Ossining, known in the vernacular as Sing Sing, just a few miles north of Manhattan. In fact, life at Dannemora was positively medieval, with none of the amenities to which Mr. Big had grown accustomed. There, this Boss of Bosses became known as Number 92169, and he was put to work in the laundry room. In short order, he went from laundering ill-gotten booty to washing other convicts' undies.

However, his influential pals on the outside saw to it that he had certain privileges.

Luciano was in Dannemora during the time of World War II and, as you'll learn in number 62, Meyer Lansky convinced the U.S. government that Luciano would be a useful resource in the war effort, given his connections to Sicily. And so, because of his service in the cause of U.S. espionage, Luciano caught a break and got relocated to Great Meadows Prison in Comstock, New York, which was a veritable pleasure cruise compared to his stint in Dannemora.

While incarcerated in Great Meadows, Lucky Luciano was granted gourmet meals, plenty of booze, and even the pleasure of female companionship. He also expected an early release from prison as a reward for his contribution to the war effort. It is ironic that the man who had him locked up, Thomas Dewey, was also the man who commuted Luciano's sentence.

Those who saw the movie *Goodfellas* will recall the scene where the head of the Lucchese crime family is enjoying gourmet meals and fine wine while doing a stretch in the slammer. Clandestine conjugal couplings with Mafiosi's *comare* (the "other woman") were also arranged. Guards and other prison officials were often easily bribed and/or intimidated. It is another regrettable example of the disparity between the haves and have-nots. Small-time criminals suffer the full weight of the penal system; those with money and means on the outside are able to use that influence on the inside to enjoy creature comforts while staying safe and unmolested in an otherwise brutal and violent environment.

What's in a nickname?

Who knows why people have a fondness for the Mafia? Maybe it has something to do with the abundance of cutesy nicknames they give one another. Some of these are terms of endearment, while others are insults. Either way, they all belong to bad guys. A mobster may be nicknamed "Winnie the Pooh," but rest assured he is after more than a jar of honey, and if you get in his way he will give you a lot more than a mere rumbly in the tumbly.

Jimmy "the Gent" Burke was no gentleman. Joe "Buddha" Manri was most likely not a student of Eastern religions and most definitely did not follow a philosophy of nonviolence. And, although we don't know the eating habits or table manners of Joseph "Joe Pig" Pignatelli, how Frankie "The Wop" Manzo got his nickname is a politically incorrect no-brainer. We can also easily infer why a certain man was called Tommy "Three Fingers" Brown, just as we can make an educated guess that Frank "Lefty" Rosenthal and Ben "Lefty Guns" Ruggiero were not right-handed.

Sometimes, a gangster's physical characteristics inspired his nickname. Jack "Handsome Jack" Giordano, Jackie "Nose" D'Amico, Anthony "Fat Tony" Salerno, Amato "Baldo" Baldassare, Ronnie "Balloon Head" DeAngelis, and Gaeton "Horsehead" Scafidi are just a few examples who fit that bill.

These wise guys were also no doubt aptly named: Sam "Mad Sam" DeStefano, Albert "The Mad Hatter" Anastasia, Ben "Bugsy" Siegel, Carl "Toughy" DeLuna, Donald "The Wizard of Odds" Angelini, Michael "Iron Mike" DeFeo, Willie "Ice Pick" Alderman, and Anthony Joseph "Joe Batters" Accardo.

But you have to wonder how and why these fellas got their names: Otto "Abbadabba" Berman, Angelo "Sonny Bamboo" McConnach, Anthony "Tony the Ant" Spilotro, Sally "Paintglass" D'Ottavio, Alphonse "Funzi" Tarricone, William "Potatoes" Daddano, Stefano "Stevie Beef" Cannone, Benny "Eggs" Mangano, Peter "Pete the Crumb" Caprio, Carmine "The Snake" Persico, John "No Nose" DiFronzo, Frank "The Dasher" Abbandando, Vito "Socko" Gurino, Joseph "Joey Doves" Aiuppa,

Salvatore "Sally Fruits" Farrugia, Antonio "Boots" Tomasulo, James "Jimmy Legs" Episcopia, Anthony "Mr. Fish" Rabito, Richie "The Boot" Boiardo, Frank "Buzzy" Carrone, Martin "Motts" Cassella, Michael "Trigger Mike" Coppola, Anthony "Tony Ducks" Corallo, Michael "The Falcon" Falciano, Carmine "Charlie Wags" Fatico, Joseph "Joe Jelly" Gioelli, Frank "Frankie the Beard" Guidice, and Phillip "Philly Broadway" Cestaro.

Still fascinated by the wacky world of Mafia nicknames? Give yourself and your friends Mafia nicknames by plugging your names in a "Mafia nickname generator" at: *www.reevo.com/newname/mafia.php.*

54

Life imitates art

The Sopranos offers a new Mafia for the New Age. The old Warner Brothers gangster movies of the 1930s presented an image of hoodlums that suited those allegedly simpler times. (The "golden age" of gangster movies ended with the release of *High Sierra* in 1941.) Perhaps the times were not so simple in real life, but the movies portrayed them as such, in much the same way that a conversation with your grandparents is likely to have them waxing nostalgic about the "good old days."

The Untouchables television show continued that classic gangster tradition with archetypal good guys and bad guys. Often the gangsters were given more complexity, but basically things were black and white with only the occasional shades of gray.

The hip, edgy *Sopranos* changed all that. Take a typical *Sopranos* episode, let's say the one that involves Tony Soprano's weekend in New England escorting his teenage daughter to open houses at exclusive, ritzy colleges. While casing out the groves of academe, Tony happens to recognize an informant who squealed on the Mafia and entered the Witness Protection Program. While keeping an eye on his daughter, conferring with a low-level hood back home, and checking in with his wife back in Jersey, Tony manages to settle the Mafia's score with the squealer, stalking and eventually murdering the rat by the end of the episode. Meanwhile, Tony's frustrated wife invites a cute young Catholic priest over for dinner and a movie, which triggers some unconsummated sexual tension.

The family man with everyday family and business problems is a common figure in television drama. Mob shows usually emphasize the criminal lives of their characters. This juxtaposition of the two worlds appeals to the millions of *Sopranos* fans.

They say that imitation is the sincerest form of flattery, and modern-day Mafiosi are the biggest fans of *The Sopranos*. FBI wiretaps reveal New Jersey's DeCavalcante Mafia family feels that they are finally getting the respect they deserve because of the hit show, which they believe is based on them. (See number 37 for more on the DeCavalcantes.) They always did have an inferiority complex, given that the New York families got all the press and all the attention for so many years. The DeCavalcantes now believe they "have arrived." They can be heard on tape taking delight in the show, pointing out landmarks in their neighborhood, and offering favorable critiques of the characterizations and the acting.

It's a good thing Lucky Luciano and the other boys from back in the day were not there to see their heirs finding validation from a television show. The old Mafia objected to *The Untouchables*; the new breed is wild about *The Sopranos*.

Mafia hypocrisy

Goodfellas, the movie based on the true story of Henry Hill and the Lucchese crime family, shows us the inherent hypocrisy of the Mafia. The men are Old-World traditionalists who claim to treasure family values, but they all have girlfriends on the side. Heaven help the wife who may indulge in extramarital dalliances. This just goes to show that, in addition to their many other vices, Mafiosi are notorious male chauvinists, too.

It is practically a given that a Mafioso has a mistress. She is the one he squires about town and lavishes with gifts while the wife, no longer an object of desire, stays home with the kids.

Mafia wives are not ideal pinup models for a National Organization for Women calendar. They stand by their man and opt to live in a state of denial about what their husbands do for a living. They take the credo "What you don't know can't hurt you" to heart. Many get accustomed to a certain lifestyle for themselves and their children, and they do not want to see it end. There are no doubt cracks in the denial and they fear for themselves and their children. If a Mafioso brings his work home with him, it can be a very messy state of affairs.

Speaking of affairs, as mentioned in number 52, the "other woman" is called a *comare* in Mafia lingo. Although most mobsters can't even spell "Sigmund Freud," they are, nevertheless, classic examples of men who are afflicted with the "Madonna/Whore syndrome." This has nothing to do with the Material Girl. This psychological trait prompts men to divide women into two camps: objects of purity and objects of lust, with no gray area in between. The girlfriends enjoy the high life, but there is no future with their sugar-daddy gangster. Meanwhile, the Mafia wives sublimate their sexual longings into other things, commiserate with other emotionally abandoned wives, and pretend that all is well.

But you can only pretend for so long. A Mafioso's business is like the elephant in the living room, an analogy often used to describe addiction in a family full of denial. Though everyone does their best to gingerly step around the elephant, and no one dares comment on it, the elephant is there, nonetheless. And it will periodically trumpet and rampage, destroying everything in its path. Such is the life of a Mafia wife.

Who put the "Scar" in "Scarface"?

When saloons became illegal during the Prohibition Era, they went underground and became "speakeasies." Now there was an illicit element that made drinking more attractive. People did not stop drinking during Prohibition. They just had to pay more money to drink (a shot of booze went up from ten cents to $3 in some places), and they had to do it in secret. But it was the worst kept secret in the nation that people still drank, and drank plenty. Some made their own alcohol, and others went to speakeasies.

Jazz, the new and uniquely American form of music, was often the music of choice, and many performers who went on to great fame got their start in the Mafia-owned nightclubs. Harlem's famous Cotton Club, owned by Irishman Owney Madden, regularly featured the likes of Duke Ellington and Cab Calloway. Ellington was even threatened with death when he tried to perform at a rival gangster's Philadelphia club. Breaking a contract with the mob was not a smart move.

Irish gangs controlled the Brooklyn waterfront after World War I. They took protection money for keeping the ships and the merchandise therein safe and sound. The Irish called themselves the "White Hand," in counterpoint to the notorious Italian "Black Hand." The leader of the White Hand was a man named Wild Bill Lovett, while Frankie Yale was the Italian leader. Both were brutal and ruthless killers. Yale also ran speakeasies and had a protégé who was rising through the ranks as a bouncer and bartender. One night, this bouncer made the mistake of telling a female patron in a speakeasy, "You got a beautiful ass." This prompted her brother to try to cut the bouncer's throat. But the man missed and sliced the bouncer's cheek instead. And that is how this chubby, outspoken tough guy, destined to become the most famous Mafioso ever, got the name Al "Scarface" Capone.

Soon enough, this verbal barroom faux pas made its way to Lucky Luciano for mediation. Capone was forced to apologize for his remark. The man who left three permanent scars on Capone's face was not obliged to say he was sorry.

Back then, it was fashionable for a gangster to have a scar or some other sign indicating that he was, indeed, a tough guy. Capone often lied about how he got the scar—and understandably so. After all, he didn't earn the scar because of hand-to-hand combat or some other macho endeavor. Nor did he get it by defending a lady's honor or something similarly gallant. Capone got his scar because he was a young punk who made a crass comment that almost got him killed. Not the stuff of which legends are born.

The Purple Gang

The city of Detroit borders Canada. A city with a river running through it, it was ideal for smuggling bootleg liquor during the wild days of Prohibition. The poor section of the city was, as is often and sadly the case, a breeding ground for juvenile delinquents. These young punks graduated from petty street crime to a more sophisticated organized crime structure after Prohibition became the law of the land. The gang that ruled the roost during this golden age was called the Purple Gang.

The Purple Gang was a group of Jewish gangsters founded by the Bernstein brothers: Abe, Joe, Raymond, and Izzy. They were not interested in rum running, as it was called. They stole the illegal booze from more experienced bootleggers. They would intercept shipments of alcohol as they arrived from over the Canadian border, and fierce battles would ensue. Its business plan was a simple one: Hijack the booze and kill the bootleggers. Since the Purple Gang was only fighting and killing other gangsters, there was little crackdown on the part of the police force. There was probably a fair amount of corruption on the force, but those cops were also likely pleased to see the bad guys bumping each other off.

Then, a couple of gangsters named Henry Shorr and Charles Leiter started mentoring these Young Turks. These men guided the Purple Gang in the finer arts of crime, and used them as muscle in dealing with their enemies. The Purple Gang also worked for corrupt labor leaders to break strikes and crack down on union rank and file when the workers demanded better treatment. This was called the Cleaners and Dyers War, named for the unions that were victimized by the gang. Beatings, bombings, and even murder were the Purple Gang's intimidation techniques of choice. Members were brought to trial but all were acquitted.

Even Al Capone was scared of the Purple Gang. Well, probably not terrified, but he elected to do business with them rather than sweep into town and clean them out. The gang members' reputation as ruthless opponents prompted Capone to make a deal with them vis-à-vis the illegal importation of booze from Canada through Detroit and down to Chicago.

Like many organizations, both legitimate and illegitimate, the Purple Gang was destroyed from within. Gang leaders killed three members because of an unsuccessful attempt to branch out on their own. These three men, Hymie Paul, Isadore Sutker, and Joe Lebowitz, were nicknamed "the Jewish Navy." They owned boats and wanted to do their own rum running and distribution, bypassing the gang. They were invited to a meeting that they were told was a peace conference, and they were murdered in cold blood. The man who drove them to the meeting was arrested and sang a very informative tune for the authorities. This resulted in the arrest and conviction of three Purple Gang kingpins: Irving Milberg, Harry Keywell, and Raymond Bernstein. They were sentenced to life in prison for what came to be known as the Collingwood Manor Massacre, named for the apartment building where the murders took place.

The Purple Gang was basically out of business by 1935. This was not the end of crime in Detroit, however. The Italian Mafia moved in and the underworld continued without missing a beat.

Made in America

In the Mafia, the main prerequisite for becoming a made man is that you have to kill someone in the course of family business. If you are willing to commit this ultimate sin with full knowledge of the potential ramifications, yet do so willingly in the service of the family, then you have the Mafia version of "the right stuff."

This is not to say that being a killer is the only requirement. Many ambitious hoods kill and kill again to no avail. But those thugs will never be welcomed into the Mafia's inner sanctum. Suffice it to say that all the gangsters who rise to the top are made men.

Take this next situation, for instance—it's a clear-cut example of upward mobility, Mafia-style. In the early 1970s, Carlo Gambino's nephew, Emmanuel "Manny" Gambino, was kidnapped and killed, and an Irish gangster by the pugnacious-sounding name of Jimmy McBratney was believed to be the killer. John Gotti curried favor with his boss Gambino by sending the errant Irishman to meet St. Patrick. It turned out that McBratney was not the killer. Gotti got the wrong guy and did two more years in the slammer, but he got in good with his boss. Around this time, Gotti had been consolidating his power base and rising within the ranks. The McBratney murder earned him the exalted position of "made" man.

Then, there's diminutive Bayou Boss Carlos Marcello. Though only five-feet-four-inches tall, he was a feisty little guy. Marcello was a "made" man in the New Orleans Mafia by the age of twenty-five.

There are many arcane rituals involved in the made-man ceremony, which hark back to Christian and Masonic rituals. One in particular involves burning the picture of a Catholic saint. Perhaps this is an inverse of the Catholic baptism ritual, where godparents, acting as the baby's spokespeople, renounce Satan and all his works.

As you read earlier in Part 1 of this book, another key component of the ceremony for made men is the taking of the omerta vow: silence. If you are made, it is assumed you will never rat out your friends. The penalty for breaking the vow of silence is—you guessed it—death.

As an interesting addendum to all this talk of becoming a made man and taking the Mafia vow of silence, Raymond Patriarca, Jr., one-time head of the Boston crime family (actually based out of Providence, Rhode Island), has an embarrassing claim to fame because he got caught on tape during an initiation ceremony. The tapes allowed outsiders, for the first time, to hear the actual ceremony during which made men were admitted into the inner sanctum. All involved went to jail.

Despite the code of omerta, there have been many rats in the mob's violent history. In the Mafia, like every other aspect of society, they just don't make 'em like they used to.

Was there a mob hit on Mario Lanza?

Mario Lanza was a popular singer who was also one of the first cross-over artists. He crossed between the worlds of opera and Hollywood, but did he cross the Mafia? And did the Mafia silence the "Voice of the Century," as he was called?

Mario Lanza was born in Philadelphia in 1921, the same year that another celebrated singer, Enrico Caruso, died. Lanza later viewed this coincidence as some kind of destiny. He was a child prodigy who did fulfill that destiny, ultimately playing the other opera star in a Hollywood biography called *The Great Caruso.*

Lanza trained as an opera singer, but in an age when Hollywood was the rage, Tinseltown beckoned and he went west. He was boffo at the box office and starred in such movies as *That Midnight Kiss, The Toast of New Orleans*, and *Because You're Mine.* Many opera fans found these films a trivialization of his talent, but Lanza reached more people with his golden voice through the movies than he would have on the stage.

Lanza lived a lavish lifestyle—he went for not only song, but wine and women as well. And let's not forget pasta. Like many opera singers, he tended toward corpulence. This was acceptable at the Met, but not in Hollywood. Legendary movie mogul Louis B. Mayer put him on a crash diet on more than one occasion, and all that yo-yoing up and down adversely affected his health. When Lanza died of a heart attack at the age of thirty-eight, while making a movie in Italy, it was attributed to his high blood pressure and high living.

But there have been rumors. Lanza had at least two run-ins with the Mafia during his short life, possibly more. His extravagance left him deeply in debt, and one day the famous boxer Rocky Marciano showed up at his door with Thomas Lucchese, don of the crime family of the same name. Lucchese offered to pay his debts in full in exchange for some concert appearances at Mafia-owned clubs. Lanza refused and curtly asked them to leave his home. He knew that you never really get out of debt when you made a deal with the Mafia. Lanza didn't make a deal that day, but he certainly made a deadly enemy.

He did not live long after he refused a Mafia kingpin for the second time. While in Italy, he turned down a request to sing at a party thrown by the exiled Lucky Luciano. Lanza was not in the best of health at the time, and he checked himself into a fancy clinic. He never checked out. He died there in 1959 of a heart attack. At least that's what the death certificate says. His wife (who died of a broken heart six months later) and one of his children believed the coronary may have been induced by the Mafia, which does not take rejection very well.

We will probably never know the true story. It sure isn't likely that there will be an *E! True Hollywood Story* about Mario Lanza any time soon. Those people are more interested in what Anna Nicole Smith and the Olsen twins are up to these days.

Femme fatale

Virginia Hill is best known as Bugsy Siegel's girlfriend at the time of his murder. Annette Bening plays Hill, opposite Warren Beatty, in the 1990 movie *Bugsy*. Prior to her relationship with Siegel, she had been linked with Al Capone, Frank Nitti, Joe Adonis, and other notorious gangsters. She was the Mafia equivalent of a rock-and-roll groupie.

But Virginia Hill was no airhead. She was a savvy, wisecracking dame straight out of film noir. She left small town Georgia in the 1930s and headed to Chicago with big dreams. She was a dancer and later an accountant for Al Capone. She had to have been clever and inventive to hold that position, since the Mafia is known for its "creative accounting" practices, but she could not save Capone from the inexorable approach and inevitable wrath of the taxman.

Hill left Chicago and went to Hollywood with big dreams in tow, but she didn't have enough talent to become a star. Her reputation as the quintessential gangster's moll preceded her, however, and she soon hooked up with Bugsy Siegel (see number 18). Virginia was with Bugsy through the Las Vegas days, and he was in her home the night he was murdered. In fact, Siegel's failed dream, the Flamingo Hotel, was named after her. That was her nickname in Mafia circles.

Some accused Bugsy of business mismanagement; others thought he was skimming from the mob and sending Hill abroad to deposit the loot in offshore accounts. Either scenario amounted to a death sentence for Siegel. The Mafia does not deal with incompetence by simply issuing a pink slip.

Although Bugsy was in Hill's apartment when he was killed, Virginia Hill was in Paris, France, at the time. Some think she may have been tipped off; others say she left town after one of their infamous heated arguments. When questioned by the cops, she played innocent, disavowing any relationship with Siegel or connection to the Mafia.

Virginia Hill remained "married" to the mob throughout her remaining post-Bugsy years. She was subpoenaed to appear before the Kefauver Committee in the early 1950s and scandalized the straight-laced politicians by responding that her sexual talents (she used a much earthier phrase) were what made her a mobster's delight.

In her last years, she settled in Switzerland. No longer an object of Mafia lust, she became concerned for her own welfare. As a woman who knew too much, she lived in fear of the Mafia and the IRS. One day she took a bottle of sleeping pills and lay down on one of the snow-covered Swiss Alps never to wake up again. There have always been rumors that her death may have been a Mafia hit. Whether or not this is actually true, the Mafia did do her in, one way or another.

61

L.A. confidential

Although the Mafia has always tried to avoid scandal, there have been many infamous instances when a gangster's name has appeared in the headlines. Capone and Gotti loved the limelight; their rises and falls were grist for the media mill. Rest assured, however, one way a macho Mafioso does not want to be publicly remembered is for being killed by a teenage girl.

In the 1950s, Johnny Stompanato was a bodyguard for the Los Angeles–based gangster Mickey Cohen. Stompanato was also dating sultry screen siren Lana Turner. All of the above real-life individuals are minor characters in the novel and movie *L.A. Confidential*, interacting with writer James Ellroy's fictional characters.

Lana Turner was an actress with the annoying penchant (annoying to all the "nice guys" out there, that is) for falling for "bad boy" types. And a Mafia killer is certainly on anyone's top ten list of bad boys— below Adolf Hitler and Osama bin Laden, perhaps, but bad nevertheless. Turner was a lusty lady, who ultimately would marry seven times and have many more lovers. She also drank too much, which no doubt contributed to some of her bad decisions in life.

Stompanato was a good-looking former Marine who never lacked for female companionship. His gal pals were usually of the well-heeled variety—the sort of women who could keep him in the lifestyle to which he had grown accustomed. At that time, his latest flavor of the week happened to be a big movie star. He and Turner had a tempestuous relationship of passionate tiffs and equally passionate "making up." It was vigorous and volatile—a classic example of the flame that burns too brightly and, thus, all too briefly.

In 1958, during a family argument, Lana Turner's fourteen-year-old daughter Cheryl Crane stabbed Johnny Stompanato to death. Crane was eavesdropping on a fight between the lovers. Allegedly, Lana wanted to break up, and Stompanato threatened to slash her face if she did, thus ruining her film career. Needless to say, Crane must have been concerned. The girl ended up stabbing Stompanato with a ten-inch kitchen knife. She was put on trial in what was the O.J. Simpson case of the day and was found innocent. It was deemed a justified homicide.

The Mafia was outraged, but no retaliation was taken. The only thing Mickey Cohen did was release a few love letters to the press from Turner to Stompanato that had happened to come into his possession. This backfired as a public relations ploy, but Cohen claimed he was just trying to defend his friend's reputation. The letters revealed passion and love on Turner's part, which countered courtroom testimony portraying Stompanato as a "fatal attraction" psycho who forced Turner to live in fear.

Lana Turner lived to make many more movies, her daughter lived to write her memoirs, and Johnny Stompanato is remembered as the gangster who got whacked by a little girl.

There have been many milestones in the history of the Mafia. There was the foundation of the Commission, which established the modern Mafia. There was the notorious Apalachin Conference that culminated with some not-so-dapper dons dodging cow dung in an upstate New York farm community, with the feds in hot pursuit. There was the Lufthansa heist that was orchestrated by a man who was post-humously portrayed by none other than Robert De Niro and Donald Sutherland in two different dramatizations of the event. And these incidents name just a few.

Part 4

Events

Of course, there also have been many celebrated hits to remind the public that the Mafia is out there doing its dirty dealings not too far from the friendly confines of their hearths and homes. This section will introduce you to some intriguing, chilling, and even humorous events in Mafia history.

62

The enemy of my enemy is my friend

Believe it or not, the American government actually formed an alliance with the Mafia during World War II. Before Italy switched sides and joined the Allies in 1943, it was allied with Nazi Germany. Benito Mussolini, Italy's fascist dictator, had made many enemies among the Sicilian Mafia. As a result, the old political adage "the enemy of my enemy is my friend" suddenly applied to relations between the United States government and the Mafia. Meyer Lansky let it be known that Lucky Luciano would be of valuable assistance in the war effort. It was suggested that Luciano could help with espionage in Sicily and help keep the New York waterfront safe from the threat of Nazi saboteurs. Sabotage was a serious threat, and who better than the gangsters who ruled the docks to "police" them for the government?

Because Thomas Dewey had busted him on prostitution charges, Luciano was serving time in Clinton State Prison, also known as Dannemora, in upstate New York. During the war years, Luciano was moved to Great Meadows Prison in Comstock, New York. This was a Club Med compared to the dank Dannemora and it was a reward for his cooperation with the government. From this new base of operations, Luciano continued to run his underworld enterprises. He also helped the Office of Naval Intelligence by providing information about German military activity on the island of Sicily. Military intelligence agents made numerous clandestine trips to Luciano's prison cell to secure his assistance.

The Mafia was happy to oblige with helping the government battle the Italian dictator. Mussolini's government had cramped the Mafia's style for over a decade, and Mafiosi would have been glad to see the dictator ousted. Ironically, when the American and British forces eventually did liberate Sicily, they also released hundreds of Mafiosi from Sicilian prisons, mistaking them for political prisoners of the fascist government.

No doubt the U.S. government wasn't aware of these men's criminal tendencies, possibly assuming that, with the exception of those who were clearly "common" criminals, most of the people Mussolini rounded up were probably political prisoners jailed for being freedom fighters. Regardless of whether or not American leadership knew that these prisoners were Mafiosi, in either case, the Mafia benefited from the Allied liberation of Sicily and returned to prominence in Sicilian society.

63

The Castellemmarese War

This infamous bout among the Mustache Petes, which pitted Salvatore Maranzano against Joe Masseria, was a brutal free-for-all that went the distance. The battle left fifty known dead, though that number is probably much higher, since the Mafia is not known for reporting its homicide statistics to the public at large. Masseria thought it was going to be a breeze. He had more men and means than the younger upstart and his Sicilian sidekicks. But the ruthless and determined Sicilian underdogs led by Maranzano gradually wrested more and more power in the violent struggle. This is where Lucky Luciano, who was working for Masseria at the time, comes in. Luciano was, in a twisted sort of way, an insightful man of vision. He believed that Masseria and the other Mustache Petes were squandering great opportunities on account of their Old-World prejudices and their reluctance to adapt to changing times.

Lucky Luciano was an ambitious young gangster who had an American mindset and approach to crime. He thought outside the Mafia box, wanted to expand the activities of the mob beyond simply business as usual, and was willing to work with criminals of other ethnicities. He was downright liberal as gangsters go. He took one look at the warring factions and decided to play the two sides against each other to his own advantage. Luciano dreamed of establishing a "commission" of crime syndicates on a national level with—who else?—himself as the Big Kahuna. This confederation was something unimaginable to the narrow-minded Mustache Petes.

Luciano ingratiated himself to Maranzano while still working for Masseria. He agreed to hit Masseria in exchange for taking control of his rackets. Luciano arranged to meet Masseria at an Italian restaurant in the Coney Island section of Brooklyn. Masseria felt safe there. He knew the owner and he knew the turf. When Luciano went to the bathroom, four men entered and blasted Masseria into the next dimensional plane, where only he knows how his Higher Power received him. The cops questioned Luciano, but he feigned innocence. One Mustache Pete down, one more to go.

Lucky Luciano had made a secret deal with Maranzano to whack Masseria, but Masseria was only half of Luciano's business plan. Maranzano was now *capo di tutti capi* (the boss of all bosses). He summoned mobsters from all over the country for a convention. They decked the halls with religious iconography to fool the feds and any other law enforcement officials who might want to crash the party. It was not a meeting of the Holy Rosary Society.

At this meeting, the plan for what became "the five families" was developed, with Maranzano at the top. His six VPs—Joseph Bonanno, Phil and Vincent Mangano, Charlie Luciano, Joseph Profaci, and Tom Gagliano—would head five families, or criminal households. But the

Mafia has always been a backstabbing bunch, and so even though this very business-like plan had been hashed out, heads were about to roll. Soon after this arrangement was made, Maranzano created a hit list that named most of his top lieutenants, including Lucky Luciano. He knew that one or more of these Young Turks was probably already plotting to usurp him. The slated shooter was a particularly nasty killer aptly named Vincent "Mad Dog" Coll. (For more on Mad Dog, see number 31.) In this instance, Luciano was as lucky as ever. He got wind of the conspiracy and took pre-emptive measures.

Luciano found out that he and Vito Genovese were to be summoned to Maranzano's office, where Coll would be waiting to "off" them. He also learned that the long arm of the Internal Revenue Service had set its sights on Maranzano. His organization was to be the subject of an IRS audit.

So Luciano sent four hit men to Maranzano's office posing as IRS accountants, and they killed Maranzano and his bodyguards in a massacre. Mr. Lucky also arranged the elimination of forty or so rivals nationwide. The era of the Mustache Petes was over, and Luciano was now the boss of all bosses.

Luciano, perhaps having been influenced by American democracy and corporate structure, rejected the title. He resolved that the five families would remain intact and, along with Meyer Lansky, formed the National Crime Syndicate, also known as the Commission. The Commission served as the structure of organized crime in America for the rest of the Mafia's glory days. Supposedly, it still exists, albeit in a somewhat less potent form. (See number 73 for more on the five families.)

The Apalachin meeting

During its heyday, the Commission met regularly every five years. At these Commission meetings, members would discuss business, amend grudges, settle debts, and make peace if necessary. Needless to say, members kept the locations private. Only the invitees and their close confidantes knew the meeting locale.

In 1957, the meeting was held in upstate New York, at Pennsylvania mobster Joseph Barbara's estate in Apalachin. This conference turned out to be one of the most infamous and embarrassing moments in Mafia history. During the meeting, Mafiosi revealed themselves as gangs that just couldn't think straight. This fiasco put the Mafia squarely in the national spotlight—a place that most Mafiosi had previously been careful to avoid.

Law enforcement officials had been trying for years to identify the heads of the big Mafia families. They wanted to get a handle on the secret society's power structure and its chain of command.

The Mafia unwittingly obliged them by gathering every major don under one roof. There was no existing agenda or itinerary for what was to be discussed at that meeting. Maybe it was the controversial drug-dealing dilemma. Perhaps the recent murder of Albert Anastasia and bungled hit on Frank Costello were the top orders of business. None of the gentlemen in attendance deigned to discuss the affair. They probably did not have a chance to discuss much, since the meeting ended rather abruptly.

Unbeknownst to Joe Barbara, he had been under surveillance for some time. Barbara (like the woman's first name) had received visits in the past from Joe Bonanno and others whom the cops suspected as criminals. Barbara had also booked most of the hotel rooms in the small town of Apalachin. These things raised a red flag for the state police.

When the convention rolled around, dons, assorted bodyguards, and wiseguys all descended upon the sleepy little community. All the goombahs dressed in pinstriped suits who flooded the area must have looked a little conspicuous in a land of cows and cornfields. The local police sensed something was afoot, and they alerted higher authorities. On November 14, 1957, four law enforcement officers pulled up to Barbara's house in two cars. The dons assumed it was a raid and scampered into the woods in a less-than-dignified fashion. The wiseguys flew out of every available egress. Some ran off into the woods. Those who escaped by car were nabbed at roadblocks and became the overnight guests of the New York State Police. All of these guys maintained that

they were paying a call on their sick friend Joe Barbara. Barbara himself told the law that it was a convention of salesmen from the Canada
Dry soft drink company.

Several sources offer different reasons for why the meeting was
called in the first place. Joe Valachi said it was a coming-out party for
the new dons, including Carlo Gambino. The gangsters were also there
to grant clemency to Vito Genovese for his role in the Anastasia murder.
(The Mad Hatter was so despised and feared that no one was particularly sorry to see him go.)

The brother of the late and not especially lamented Anastasia, who
went by the name Anastasio, said that the objective of the meeting was
to decide which misbehaving mobsters and which intrusive federal
agents were to be whacked. Still another theory is that the whole thing
was designed to set up and embarrass Vito Genovese, and the police
were tipped off about the meeting. (Genovese was sent to prison on
drug charges less than a year later.)

The names of those detained in this debacle form a who's who
of hoodlums: Carlo Gambino, Paul Castellano, Tommy Lucchese, Joe
Profaci, Joe Colombo, Vito Genovese, Frank Costello, Tony Accardo,
Santos Trafficante, Carlos Marcello, and Sam Giancana.

Believe it or not, none of the approximately sixty dons were arrested, only detained for questioning. So little was known about the shadowy Mafia in 1957 that the cops had no idea they had, in one fell swoop,
just nabbed the most vicious and successful criminal kingpins in the

country. Despite the dearth in arrests, this bust served an important purpose: The shadow life of the Mafia was over.

After the Apalachin meeting, the Mafia was no longer a badly kept secret or a word uttered only in a hushed, fearful whisper. Dons were on the covers of *Life* and *Look* magazines. The media was abuzz with all things Mafia, and even FBI Director J. Edgar Hoover had to admit that it existed.

Despite this admission, the FBI under the directorship of Hoover did very little to combat organized crime, as you will see in Part 5. Hoover knew many reputed gangsters and was a bigtime horse player. He was either in denial, or in collusion with the Mafia. (See number 84.)

From this point on, the Mafia entered American popular culture as a subject of fascination, outrage, and revulsion. Never again would the activities of these ruthless and brutal men remain completely in the shadows. The Mafia was now as famous as it was infamous, and its world was no longer an inner sanctum of clandestine criminality. The law turned up the heat, and the public loved to read about their exploits and see movies about them. In the aftermath, Mafiosi would do the unthinkable and break their sacred vow of omerta. Even some Mafiosi themselves would be swept away in their celebrity status. A prime example of this is our next subject, the infamous "Dapper Don," John Gotti. He was ultimately his own worst enemy and did more damage to himself and the Mafia than any informant or crusading crime fighter.

65

Little boy lost

The tragic story of the death of John Gotti's son is worth telling because of what it says about Mafia justice. In March 1980, John Gotti's twelve-year-old son, Frank, was puttering around the family's Howard Beach, Queens, neighborhood when he was struck and killed by a car. The driver, John Favara, was a neighbor of the Gottis. Favara's son and little Frank Gotti were friends. They even had sleepovers at each other's homes. It was a terrible tragedy and clearly an accident.

Shortly thereafter, Favara began receiving death threats. Although the local police suggested that he move, he did not take these threats seriously at first. After all, Frank's death had been an accident.

When the word *MURDERER* was spray-painted on Favara's car, one of his friends, the son of an old mobster, urged him "to take a powder"—slang for hastily leaving the scene. Even then, Favara was reluctant to leave, but after Gotti's wife, Victoria, attacked him with a baseball bat, he changed his mind. He put his house up for sale and decided to get out of town.

Favara did not get very far. He simply disappeared one morning, never to be heard from again. Veteran crime reporter Jerry Capeci pieced the story together many years after the fact. According to

Capeci, witnesses saw Favara get clubbed and thrown into a van. But because these witnesses were intimidated, they had remained silent. It is believed that Favara's body ended up at the bottom of the Atlantic Ocean, after being dumped in a barrel that was filled with cement. The offending automobile was turned into scrap metal. Another slightly different version of the story has Favara receiving a grisly execution by chainsaw. His remains were then put in his car, which was compressed to the size of a one-square-foot slab of metal.

Mr. and Mrs. Gotti were in Florida when these events transpired. They were questioned upon their return, but as usual, there was no evidence to link them to Favara's disappearance. John Gotti did volunteer the unsolicited opinion that if something bad did befall Favara, it was no skin off his Cosa Nostra.

The Mafia's rise during Prohibition

America's experiment with Prohibition in the 1920s opened the door for the Mafia to make a bundle trafficking illegal booze. As a result, the mob hit its heyday. Humankind has been consuming alcohol ever since the first caveman left grape juice lying around too long, and then realized he got a pleasant buzz when he drank it. While not a problem when imbibed in moderation, without a doubt, the abuse of alcohol has destroyed many people's lives, and the lives of their loved ones.

Throughout history, there have been many attempts to deal with the problem of alcoholism. These were called temperance movements, an antiquated phrase meaning moderation of one's indulgence in the so-called vices. Religious folks who felt that only a spiritual conversion could combat the deleterious effects of "demon rum" have initiated most of these temperance movements. Many groups have even wanted to ban all alcoholic beverages from the American landscape.

In the late nineteenth century, the temperance movement in America became increasingly popular and influential. It was sometimes called the "Women's War," since most of its members were women who were fed up with their drunken fathers, husbands, and sons. At that time, the Anti-Saloon League (ASL) gained popularity in many states. The ASL endorsed candidates and tried to influence state and local governments, and its dream was to have an impact at the national level.

The National Prohibition Act was passed to enforce the Eighteenth Amendment. It was also known as the Volstead Act, named for the congressman who introduced the law. Prohibition became the law of the land in 1920. Ironically, the 1920s was, for many Americans, the last big party before the Great Depression of the 1930s. The booze never stopped flowing during Prohibition, thanks to the friendly neighborhood Mafia families.

The Mafia both manufactured illegal alcohol and brought it over the border from Canada, Mexico, and the Caribbean. Off the coast of Philadelphia, for example, ships with bootleg booze lingered in international waters, and small boats went out to meet them to collect the booty. It was all done more or less in the open. The Coast Guard was not immune to bribery, and enterprising small-craft owners even took tourists out to watch the bootleggers at work. The booze that came off the boats was quality vintage from Europe, Canada, and elsewhere. The Philadelphia mob boss with the infantile nickname "Boo Boo" Hoff was also involved in making local moonshine, with sometimes fatal results. He got involved with a couple of industrial alcohol companies and had the alcohol redistilled for human consumption. The process was less than perfect, and sometimes the product was more poisonous than rubbing alcohol. People suffered blindness and death from drinking "bathtub gin." The mercenary rationalization of many moonshiners was that all they did was sell it. What people did with it was their business.

The mayor of Philadelphia brought in a former Marine with the Dickensian name of Smedley Darlington Butler to clean up the town. After two years and little cooperation from local law enforcement and the political machine, Butler was unable to oust Boo Boo Hoff, and he left in a huff.

Just say yes

For years the Mafia had a love-hate relationship with the world of illegal drugs. Although the Mafia proclaimed its unwillingness to get involved with drugs, it always was, at least to some extent, embroiled in the business. Finally, the allure of the big money became too great, and drug operations came to play a larger role in the Mafia's business.

Contrary to what many people believe, drug use in America did not begin with the hippies in the 1960s. Drugs have been popular since humans first discovered the natural kick certain chemicals and plants contain, and then learned to refine them for greater potency.

In the late nineteenth century, opium dens were easy to find. Patrons could go into these dimly lit, seedy establishments, usually run by Chinese immigrants, smoke opium, recline on a cot, and enjoy their drug-induced reverie. There were also numerous opium-based drugs openly sold in the marketplace. In fact, children's medication was often laced with opium.

When opium was outlawed in 1875, addicts turned to a legal substitute—heroin. Yes, heroin was once legal in the United States. In 1898, the Bayer Pharmaceutical Company actually touted heroin as a nonaddictive substitute for the highly addictive painkiller morphine.

Astoundingly, even Coca-Cola was laced with cocaine for a time during the nineteenth century. Drugs have always been around, and there has always been a subculture of addicts.

The American government made its first attempt to control narcotics use when it implemented the Harrison Narcotics Act of 1914. This act did not do much good, however. It required businesses that dealt in opium and cocaine products to register with the federal government, and taxed them a penny per ounce on items they shipped through the United States postal service. Doctors were allowed to dispense heroin, opium, and morphine to patients "for medicinal purposes." This resulted in the earliest versions of rehab centers. Like the methadone clinics of later decades, these facilities tried to break people's morphine addiction by giving them heroin. But morphine addiction became a serious problem for many American soldiers during World War I, so in 1923, the Supreme Court made it illegal for doctors to prescribe heroin and morphine for any reason. Making these drugs illegal didn't end the scourge of drug addiction in America; it simply drove drug trafficking underground. Enter the Mafia, which was all too ready, willing, and able to take up the slack and make billions of dollars over the remainder of the twentieth century. Although Mafiosi outwardly acted as if drug trafficking was beneath them, in private they greedily salivated at the money to be made. The New Orleans Mafia was already dealing drugs, including marijuana, in the nineteenth century. (Marijuana was popular in the local African-American community in turn-of-the-century New

Orleans.) Although the Mafia talked a lot about keeping drugs away from children and from Italian and Sicilian neighborhoods, it didn't much care if those same drugs destroyed individuals from other ethnic groups. (In addition to its deep insularity, the Mafia always had a nasty racist streak, too.)

Unlike their Southern counterparts, the Mafia crime families in the North were slower to jump on the narcotics bandwagon. The old guard from the Old World wanted nothing to do with drugs. There was plenty of money to be made in the bootlegging, gambling, and prostitution rackets. These were regarded as harmless vices by many people, even law enforcement officials, who often turned a blind eye, even when these activities went on right under their noses.

Drug trafficking was another matter altogether. When the Young Turks wiped out the old guard in the Castellemmarese War, the new and Americanized leaders of the Mafia reconsidered the mob's decision to stay out of the drug trade. As the old dons died and the Young Turks took over, they were less concerned about the nasty nature of the drug trade and more interested in the profits to be made.

The northern Mafia families already had a peripheral role in the narcotics business anyway. Their Jewish pals—Meyer Lansky, Dutch Schultz, Legs Diamond, and others—were involved in the heroin business in the 1920s. The new boss of bosses, Lucky Luciano, decided that the Italians should get a piece of the action.

When Prohibition was repealed in 1933, after the election of

Franklin Delano Roosevelt, the Mafia turned its sights on the heroin racket. The decision made good business sense. Though there were fewer drug addicts than drinkers in the country, the profit margin would be much higher, and drugs would be easier to smuggle. Packets of powder do not noisily clink-clank in crates as they are unloaded off ships in the dead of night.

And Lucky Luciano was one of the masterminds behind the Mafia's increased business in drug trafficking. United States officials thought they were getting rid of a rotten apple when they deported Lucky Luciano back to Italy in 1946. Turns out, they should have left him in the slammer, because during his exile in Italy, Lucky Luciano masterminded the modern heroin trade. More recently, the dumbed-down dons have adapted to the times, and the drug trade has become a much more open part of Mafia business. The Mafia's pretense of civility and its vaunted code of honor gave way to the inherent greed of its members. Ultimately, the Mafia went from avoiding involvement in narcotics, to involvement with reservations, to outright and enthusiastic drug trafficking.

68

Old Blue Eyes as the Godfather?

Imagine Frank Sinatra, George C. Scott, or Laurence Olivier as Don Corleone. How about Jack Nicholson as favorite son Michael Corleone, or Burt Reynolds as the volatile Sonny Corleone? All of these actors at one time expressed interest in or were considered for those roles in *The Godfather.*

In the 1960s, Mario Puzo's novel *The Godfather,* one of the most talked about bestsellers of the time, introduced millions of voracious readers to the world of La Cosa Nostra. The film version was inevitable, and it and its two sequels became an American epic. Some thought these films glorified the mob and were too sympathetic in their portrayal. There is no denying that these popular movies may have put forth a classier treatment than the wise guys deserved.

The Godfather may have been an entirely different experience if some of the other actors considered for the roles had been cast. Frank Sinatra as Don Corleone? Often linked to the mob and unfairly pegged as the inspiration for the notorious "horse's head" scene in the first *Godfather* movie, Sinatra physically attacked novelist Puzo in a restaurant after the novel was published. Apparently he got over it, because a few years later he expressed interest in playing the role of the Godfather.

Actor Robert Duvall, who played consigliere Tom Hagen, was present at Laurence Olivier's audition and noted the venerable thespian's subtle, nuanced performance and his attention to detail in mastering the perfect Sicilian accent. George C. Scott, fresh off his Oscar-winning turn as the titular *Patton*, said in an interview many years later that his vanity prevented him from pursuing the role. He did not want to play someone so much older than he.

Of course, that coveted role went to Marlon Brando, who proved to be his usual cranky and difficult self on the set. Nevertheless, he managed to mumble his way to an Academy Award, which he ostentatiously refused to accept.

The Godfather made Al Pacino a star. He went on to play numerous other gangster roles, including non-Italian hoodlums in *Scarface* and *Carlito's Way*. But can you imagine Robert Redford or Ryan O'Neal as Michael Corleone? Director Francis Ford Coppola told producers he wanted someone with "the map of Sicily on his face" to play Michael. Strange indeed, but O'Neal and Redford were the producer's first choices for the part. While there are fair-haired and blue-eyed Italians, that wasn't exactly what Coppola had in mind. Fortunately, the director insisted on Pacino, and the rest, as they say, is Hollywood history.

The Dapper Don meets Grandpa Munster

The final John Gotti trial was, to no one's surprise, a media circus. His once loyal lieutenant became the most celebrated informant in Mafia history. Sammy the Bull soon became known as Sammy the Rat in the local papers. Gotti's people initiated a smear campaign, calling Gravano everything from a homosexual to a compulsive womanizer. The defense team even called a bizarre assortment of "character witnesses," including the venerable late actor Anthony Quinn, the decidedly unvenerable actor Mickey Rourke, and Al "Grandpa Munster" Lewis. The three celebs told the press and TV reporters what a great guy Gotti was.

The Mafia-Hollywood connection is a strong one. Celebrities are often fascinated by Mafiosi's "bad boy" images. Allegedly, even a tough guy like Frank Sinatra would swoon in a most unseemly manner when in the company of Mafia hoodlums. But Gotti's connection to these Hollywood characters was strange, at best. Despite the efforts of his Hollywood brigade, Gotti didn't stand a chance. When Sammy the Bull, who had been sequestered at a Marine Corps base in Virginia, took the stand during the trial, that was, as they say, all she wrote. He placed Gotti at the scene of the Paul Castellano murder and fingered him as the man who orchestrated the hit.

In 1992, Gotti was convicted and sentenced to life in prison, without the possibility of parole. It's believed that he continued to run things from behind bars for many years. Eventually, however, health problems took over. Gotti, who was diagnosed with cancer, lingered gravely ill for many years in a prison infirmary.

John Gotti succumbed to his illness on June 10, 2002, at the age of sixty-one. The Associated Press eulogized him as follows: "John Gotti, who swaggered, schemed, and murdered his way to the pinnacle of organized crime in America only to be toppled by secret FBI tapes and a turncoat mobster's testimony, died at a prison hospital Monday while serving a life sentence."

John Gotti delivered his own obituary right before he was sent to jail. It was certainly more colorful—and filled with hubris—than the press reports that covered his death. The Dapper Don was nothing if not full of himself. "I'll always be one of kind," he said. "You'll never see another guy like me if you live to be 5,000."

Goodbye, Colombo

Like John Gotti, mobster Joe Colombo got swept up in his celebrity and brought about his own downfall. During the Banana Wars, Carlo Gambino rewarded hit man Joe Colombo for switching sides and warning him about Joe Bonanno's plans to whack him. Colombo was made the don of the family that henceforth bore his name. While most other Mafiosi kept a very low profile, Colombo was one of those gangsters who liked the limelight. Colombo thought it would be a good idea to exploit Italian-Americans' ethnic pride by staging a series of public rallies that would equate anti-Mafia sentiment with anti-Italian racism. He accused the feds of being anti-Italian in their prosecution of the Mafia. Colombo even had the audacity to found the Italian-American Civil Rights League, an organization meant to combat the negative stereotypes that cast Italian-Americans as all having some connection to the Mafia. The Italian-American Civil Rights League's first rallies got a lot of media attention—something any levelheaded Mafioso does not want. The shrewder Mafia dons did not like the light of this publicity, as they knew it would do more damage than good. Carlo Gambino was fed up with the man he recommended as don. Gambino told Colombo to stop—or else—and Colombo refused.

In 1971, Joe Colombo caught a shot in the head while attending one of his rallies at Columbus Circle in Manhattan, right at the entrance to Central Park. The perpetrator was an African-American gangster named Jerome A. Johnson. Before he could make a hasty retreat, a police officer at the crime scene promptly shot—and killed—Johnson. At the time, police believed Johnson was the "lone gunman," but this was not the case. He was working for Gambino, and did not expect to be the patsy, or fall guy. This is a conspiracy that, on a small scale, mirrors the alleged conspiracy surrounding the murder of President John Kennedy, in which the Mafia often pops up as an alleged participant. (The hit man was supposedly a lone gunman, but it became immediately clear that he was hired by the mob and set up to take the fall. If such a scenario can be accepted on this small scale, why is it a stretch for many people to accept that the same thing could have possibly occurred on a grander scale—with the murder of a President?)

Joe Colombo did not die immediately. The once powerful Mafia don suffered what would be for anyone, much less a macho mobster, a terrible and ignominious fate. He lingered in a vegetative coma for seven years before finally dying.

The don is dead—long live the don

Paul Castellano, a.k.a. Big Paulie, got a big surprise the day he walked the few paces from his car to Sparks Steak House in Manhattan. It was December 1985, and Christmas shoppers crowded the busy city sidewalks, dressed in holiday style. Right there in the open, four gunmen administered six bullets to Castellano's head, just to be on the safe side. Shortly thereafter, John Gotti cruised by in a passing car and surveyed the carnage. Another Mafia transfer of power had been successfully staged. John Gotti was the Big Boy now.

It seems Big Paulie had gotten himself into some hot water. In the early 1980s, the government was aggressively pursuing the heads of the five New York crime families. They were being prosecuted under charges that came to be called RICO (Racketeer Influenced and Corrupt Organizations). Castellano learned that he was going to be indicted in at least two RICO cases. Gotti seized upon the old don's vulnerability and began planning his demise.

When Carlo Gambino became ill in the 1970s, his underlings began jockeying for position as his heir apparent. Gambino did not choose his underboss Aniello Dellacroce, who would have been next in the chain of command, to succeed him. He instead chose his brother-in-law Paul

Castellano. He gave Dellacroce the consolation prize, control of the family's Manhattan rackets. Dellacroce's feelings were hurt. And when a sensitive mobster's feathers are ruffled, the fur usually flies. Between the time Gambino fell ill and his death in 1976, Gotti had been consolidating his power base and rising within the ranks. The murder of the Irish gangster Jimmy McBratney had helped Gotti attain the exalted position of "made" man. The heist crew that operated out of his Bergin Hunt and Fish Club were his guys now, loyal to the up-and-coming capo. However, the new boss, Paul Castellano, did not have as high an opinion of Gotti. That in itself thwarted Gotti's ambitions. Gotti, in turn, did not like or respect Castellano.

The Castellano-Dellacroce leadership was uninspired, and the Young Turk John Gotti was plotting and planning as he waited in the wings. Although the young soldiers and capos respected Dellacroce, Castellano was not held in equal esteem. When they learned that Dellacroce was dying of cancer, they waited. Castellano was murdered two weeks after Dellacroce succumbed to cancer, and John Gotti became the new don.

Castellano had not been respected as a don, and Mafia experts believe that the fact that he did not see this hit coming and take precautions reflects his incompetence.

Just a little off the top

Alfred Mineo and Steve Ferrigno were bosses of the Brooklyn crime outfit until they were murdered in 1930 by Joe Profaci and Joe Valachi, among others. The new bosses were the Mangano brothers, Vince and Phil. These guys ruled the roost until they were killed in 1951 by their ambitious and psychotic henchman Albert Anastasia, who remained boss until his famous barbershop murder in 1957.

Under Anastasia's watch, which, in turn, was under the watchful eye of Frank Costello, the crime family grew in power and stature. But Anastasia was not nicknamed "The Mad Hatter" for nothing. The very skills that made him ideal for the role of Lord High Executioner of Murder, Incorporated, were a liability in the role of don. Being a don required more subtlety and diplomacy, things Anastasia did not possess. He was a loose cannon who brought unwanted publicity to the Mafia.

Anastasia enjoyed his position as don, but his handlers had their own reasons for promoting him. Frank Costello was in the midst of a rivalry with Vito Genovese vying for control of the interests and rackets of the recently deported Lucky Luciano.

Anastasia wanted a piece of Meyer Lansky's Cuban casino action, and Lansky refused. This increased the bad blood between the two.

Lansky did not shirk from rubbing out even his closest friends, and had no compunction about taking a proactive stance against Albert Anastasia. Lansky decided he didn't want to wait for Anastasia and Genovese to solve his problem for him. He ordered a hit on the Mad Hatter.

On October 25, 1957, Anastasia went to the barbershop of the Park Sheraton Hotel in New York City. Two masked men entered, and the Lord High Executioner himself was offed in a hail of bullets. The fact that his bodyguard did not quickly join his boss in the barbershop after parking the car indicates that there was a conspiracy within Anastasia's own family, no doubt led by the man who succeeded him, Carlo Gambino. And thus the Gambino crime family came into being. Ultimately, Gambino betrayed Genovese and switched to Meyer Lansky and Frank Costello's family. Together, in 1958, they entrapped Genovese in a drug rap that sent him away for life. Genovese died in prison in 1969.

73

All in the family

When most people think of the Mafia, in addition to Al Capone's Chicago, they think of New York's five families. Indeed, in their glory days the five families were the most powerful criminal organizations in the nation. During the Castellemmarese War, Salvatore Maranzano became capo di tutti capi (the boss of all bosses). He summoned mobsters from all over the country for a convention. Although they decked the halls with religious iconography to fool the feds and any other law enforcement officials who might want to crash the party, this was no potluck Christmas celebration.

At this meeting, the Mafia hashed out its flow chart for what would become "the five families." Maranzano was the CEO, and he appointed the VPs who would head the families. The heads of the criminal households would be Joseph Bonanno, Phil and Vincent Mangano, Charlie Luciano, Joseph Profaci, and Tom Gagliano.

Despite the Mafia's supercilious claims of honor, the old adage that there is no honor among thieves is a universal truth. Luciano sent four hit men to Maranzano's office posing as IRS accountants, and they killed Maranzano and his bodyguards in a massacre.

The Bonanno, Colombo, Gambino, Genovese, and Lucchese crime families, all located in New York City, are, to this day, the most powerful organized crime units in the country. Of course there are crime families all across the country, but it is believed they report to the big bosses in New York and Chicago, with the exception of the New Orleans crime family, which remains independent of the rest.

The Mafia and the media

The Old-World Mafia men who came to our shores at the turn of the twentieth century are no doubt turning over in their graves at the behavior of their posterity. Andy Warhol is famous for saying that eventually every American will become famous for fifteen minutes, and in this celebrity-obsessed age members of the Mafia are no exception.

Of course, this sort of Mafia infamy is not an entirely recent phenomenon. Al Capone was a grandstander who loved the limelight. Press coverage and public fascination with him, along with a certain amount of support because Prohibition was very unpopular, gave him a mistaken sense of invulnerability, and that proved to be his undoing.

So, too, with John Gotti many decades later. He strutted and fretted his hour upon the stage, and then was heard no more, but not before an irresponsible media turned him into some kind of hero, something he most definitely was not.

In other lesser-known tales of Mafia notoriety, it would seem that some Mafia rats are as good in the kitchen as they are in the fine art of leg breaking. Joseph "Joe Dogs" Iannuzzi, a mob hit man turned informant, is the author of *The Mafia Cookbook: With 37 New, Foolproof Recipes to Die For.* The author-chef-gangster regales the reader with anecdotes of his violent past between recipes. And Henry Hill, rat extraordinaire of *Goodfellas* fame, wrote *The Wiseguy Cookbook: My Favorite Recipes from My Life As a Goodfella to Cooking on the Run*. Even the fictional mob is getting in on this act with *The Sopranos Family Cookbook*.

But Mafia authors do more than write cookbooks—they offer even juicier tomes. As previously mentioned, Joe Bonanno was the first head of a crime family to write a "tell all" memoir. It was not really a tell all at all—it was as self-serving as its title, *A Man of Honor*. His son Bill Bonanno followed suit with *Bound by Honor: A Mafioso's Story*. Now it is almost accepted as a given that, should a Mafioso get a certain amount of media attention, an agent will get him a book and maybe even a movie deal. And if he's lucky, not just some cheesy movie of the week, but something directed by the mighty Scorsese himself.

Why did this phenomenon occur? Perhaps it has do to with the dumbing down of American culture. Maybe "infotainment," the combination of information and entertainment, is what people really want. It's the modern version of the Roman bread and circuses philosophy.

There is a reason Meyer Lansky was nicknamed "The Brain." He kept a low profile, stayed in the shadows, lived a long life, and died of natural causes. He was ultimately played in movies by the likes of Richard Dreyfus and Sir Ben Kingsley, but this happened long after his demise and without his enthusiastic participation.

Viva Las Vegas

Las Vegas is also known as Sin City, the place where you can indulge your deepest, darkest fantasies and maybe even make your fortune. The Mafia was a fixture in Vegas during its glitzy glory days, transforming it from a wild and woolly honky-tonk town to the entertainment capital of the world.

Gambling casinos existed before the Mafia got to Las Vegas. The state of Nevada legalized gambling in 1931. The early casinos were more like rowdy honky-tonks and cowboy hangouts than the modern casinos that would soon spring up in the desolate wilderness. Who would have thought that a bunch of immigrant kids from New York's Lower East Side would become the power brokers and robber barons in the Wild West? When the Mafia decreed, "Go West, Young Hoodlum," they sent an emissary by the name of Bugsy Siegel to the Promised Land and, so the legend goes, he put Las Vegas on the map.

Siegel's role in transforming Las Vegas into the Mafia's playground has already been described in the earlier parts of this book (see number 18). When vainglorious Bugsy was out of the picture, less flamboyant but more efficient mobsters flooded Las Vegas. Meyer Lansky took over the Flamingo and had it running smoothly and profitably within a year. He also was the brains behind the Thunderbird Casino, and he controlled the Sands hotel, too, along with Frank Costello and others. The mobsters brought in Francis Albert Sinatra to attract the tourists. Sinatra's name on the marquee filled the hotel and the coffers of the clandestine criminal element from the 1950s through the '70s.

The famous Rat Pack antics, about which you read earlier, in Part 2, took place at the Sands, and the 1960 Rat Pack movie *Ocean's Eleven* was filmed by day at the casino, while the Rat Pack performed nights at the Sands. Other gangsters rounded out the roster of Las Vegas casinos secretly owned by the mob. The Cleveland mob ran the Desert Inn. Sinatra's compatriot Sam Giancana, along with the Fischetti brothers and others, had interests in the Sahara and the Riviera. The New England contingent hung their fedoras in the cloakroom of the Dunes.

Not satisfied with making money as hidden partners in the casino business, the mob had other methods for raking in the dough. The mob wouldn't be the mob if it didn't do something illegal in the world of legalized gambling. The most popular method was called skimming.

The premise was simple. When the oodles of cash and coins were collected and taken to the big casinos' "counting rooms," a certain percentage was "skimmed" off the top and sent as tribute to the big crime families back home. This was cold cash free and clear, not subject to the grasping talons of the IRS. In a cash business where the moolah was flowing, the money made via skimming was astronomical.

The Mafia's luck in Vegas began to run out, however, when the poster boy for eccentric millionaires, Howard Hughes, decided he wanted to make the town his life-size Monopoly board. Nowadays Las Vegas is more family-oriented theme park than Sin City, at least on the fabled Strip and other clean, well-lit corners of town.

By the time Hughes blew into town, the old hoods were ready for retirement anyway. They had done more than wet their beaks. They had gorged themselves on the sumptuous Las Vegas smorgasbord. It was a great run for the underworld.

The Lufthansa heist

In 1978, Jimmy "the Gent" Burke illegally broke curfew and snuck out of a halfway house for convicted felons on probation. His pal Tommy DeSimone picked him up, and the two drove from Manhattan to John F. Kennedy International Airport in Queens. Their destination was the Lufthansa terminal at Kennedy. The result of this little joyride to JFK is what has come to be known as the Lufhansa heist. In recent years, the Lufthansa heist has received lots of coverage—first in the Martin Scorsese film *Goodfellas*, and then in the made-for-cable movie called *The Big Heist*. Robert DeNiro and Donald Sutherland played the character of Burke respectively, and they each turned in very different interpretations of this character.

Fictitious portrayals aside, here's what happened in the real heist. Once at the airport, Burke and DeSimone found their partners in crime, who had already gone to work and were holding several employees captive. These men were known as the Robert's Lounge Gang, named for the bar Burke owned, where the team often planned and schemed. The heist team got away with more than $6 million in cash, money orders, traveler's checks, and jewelry. Jimmy the Gent got a ride back to the halfway house, snuck back in, and went to sleep, having just participated in one of the most infamous robberies in the history of the Mafia.

Nothing goes as smoothly as the Lufthansa heist without an inside man. A cargo supervisor named Louis Werner was heavily in debt to a Mafia loan shark and he provided the inside assistance in order to pay his debt and spare himself a pair of broken legs—or worse. The gagged and bound staff watched the gangsters remove seventy-two fifteen-pound cartons of cash and other goodies, bypassing the security systems. The members of the heist team were wearing hoods and brandishing firearms, but no one was killed during the stickup. The same cannot be said of the robbers in what was a particularly bloody aftermath to a virtually bloodless crime.

No one was ever charged for the crime and almost none of the merchandise and money was recovered, but almost all of the perpetrators ended up dead or in jail. It is alleged that Burke became greedy and began bumping off those who participated in the robbery.

So how does Henry Hill—the now-famous character Ray Liotta portrayed in *Goodfellas*—fit into all of this? Hill, who was not present at the actual Lufthansa robbery but had been in on the planning, was no stranger to airport heists. In 1968, with help from an inside source, he walked into an Air France office at Kennedy airport and walked out with a suitcase full of $480,000 in cash. This time around, Hill was worried about becoming another name on the growing list of murdered and mysteriously missing Mafiosi. So Henry Hill turned on his buddies and sent Burke and Lucchese crime boss Paul Vario packing—straight to the slammer, that is. Both died there.

Did the Mafia kill Superman?

The Mafia has done many terrible things in its long and nefarious history. But did it really kill Superman?

George Reeves played Superman in the 1950s television series *The Adventures of Superman*. The series ran for six years, making Reeves a popular star and cementing his place in pop-culture legend.

Sadly, all good things must come to an end, and in 1957 *The Adventures of Superman* was canceled. Like many an actor who becomes thoroughly identified with the part he plays, George Reeves found himself typecast as Superman. Other parts were not forthcoming because producers felt the audience would only see Superman on screen, not the actor Reeves playing a different character. In this way, the pressures of being Superman took their toll on Reeves. Eventually, it led to depression, heavier drinking (by all accounts, Reeves already drank too much), and finally, in the wee hours of June 16, 1959—three days before his scheduled wedding day—his suicide.

Or was it a suicide? The coroner's report determined that Reeves' death was caused by a single gunshot to the head—self-inflicted. On the day of his death, Reeves, his fiancée, and a few friends were boozing it up in his home. He went upstairs, and shortly thereafter a shot was heard. No one saw or heard anyone else, but everyone present was under the influence. Needless to say, they weren't the most reliable witnesses. The case was closed, but there is enough compelling evidence to cast more than a shadow of doubt in the Mafia's direction.

In the years before his possible murder, Reeves had had an affair with a married woman. Not just any married woman. She was married to a Hollywood producer who was known for being well connected with the Mafia. When Reeves ended the affair, shortly before his death, the scorned woman pulled a "fatal attraction" and began to harass Reeves. Though this theory has never been proven, it is believed that this woman even kidnapped and killed Reeves's beloved dog. She was mad at him, and her husband was mad at him. Not to mention that Reeves's fiancé was also a jealous and unstable woman. There was no shortage of suspects in this suspicious case.

Despite these hazardous romantic entanglements, Reeves's life did seem to be taking a turn for the better in certain other ways at this time. Reeves's career was on the upswing again: There was going to be a new season of *The Adventures of Superman*, and he was also headed to Spain to make a movie. His slump appeared to be over, which makes his apparent suicide all the more curious. Then there is the forensic evidence. There were no fingerprints on the gun. How could he have wiped the weapon clean after shooting himself in the head? There were also no gunpowder marks on his forehead, indicating that the gun was fired from several inches away from his head—not pressed against his temple. The location of the gun, on the floor, was also inconsistent with a self-inflicted gunshot.

Given these dubious details, many believe that it was Reeves's jilted lover, her husband with gangster ties, or an individual from the Mafia hired who killed Superman. Whatever the case may be, there is a very strong probability that, directly or indirectly, the Mafia had a hand in the murder of this popular television star.

Sicily, USA

Before Alaska and Hawaii became the forty-ninth and fiftieth states to join the Union, certain members of the Mafia would have liked to see Sicily become one of the United States of America.

As reported elsewhere in this book (see number 62), Lucky Luciano was released from prison in the United States with the understanding that he would help the Americans battle the Germans on Sicilian soil during World War II. Luciano had plenty of connections with the Sicilian Mafia, which was not functioning well under Benito Mussolini's dictatorship. The Mafia was also rooting for the Americans because their business would be more prosperous in a democracy than under a dictatorship. Some Mafiosi even wanted to take things a step further and have Sicily join the Union. Thus, a separatist movement was born to sever the island of Sicily from mainland Italy.

The Mafia worked with the Allies at the bureaucratic and political level in the postwar years. U.S. forces placed Mafia members in positions of authority. But every revolutionary movement needs a heroic figure; in this case that man was a Robin Hood-like bandit named Salvatore Giuliano. He was a violent criminal, but not part of the Mafia. In fact, the Mafia did not like this independent freelancer.

Guiliano was no angel. He killed those who betrayed him, and because of those killings, he headed straight for the hills to escape the law. But when he stole, he only robbed from the rich. And he actually did give to the poor. Hence, the Robin Hood label.

The Mafia, Giuliano, and other political activists in Sicily proved that politics and the mob do indeed make strange bedfellows, when they formed the MIS (Movement for Sicilian Independence) and ran their fledgling party in the upcoming elections. The MIS did not win. A party called the Christian Democrats were victorious instead, and after this, the Mafia's interest in the movement began to wane.

The Mafia was not involved in the movement out of patriotism. As always, the mob's interest was pragmatic and self-serving. Mafiosi feared that the Communist Party or the Socialist Party might win the election, and then they would be in almost as bad a position as they had been under Mussolini. With a democracy in Sicily and in Rome, they could conduct business with ease and did not need to become part of the United States.

After the elections, Giuliano retreated to the hills and continued his Robin Hood antics, until he was finally murdered in his bed by a friend who betrayed him. There really is no honor among thieves.

79

Jimmy Hoffa: Case closed?

One of the biggest Mafia mysteries of all time concerns Teamster Union boss Jimmy Hoffa. One night, in July of 1975, he went off to meet a few gentlemen in the organized crime community to discuss his return to the Union (he was recently released from a stint in prison), and he was never heard from again. His disappearance has entered popular culture as a source of debate and the subject of dark humor.

Recently, a man by the name of Frank Sheeran confessed to Hoffa's murder shortly before his own death. Sheeran, an old fellow living in Detroit, contacted Fox News to make his confession, but he would not allow it to be aired. While interviewing him, a Fox News reporter found traces of blood in Sheeran's house, and later the authorities did a thorough forensic examination of the man's home.

Hoffa was president of the teamsters from 1957 to 1967. He was sent to jail for jury tampering and fraud and pardoned in 1971. On the day he died, July 30, 1975, he planned to meet two gangsters, Anthony "Tony Pro" Provenzano and Tony Giacalone. Hoffa was looking for financial support to help win back presidency of the union. Sheeran accompanied Hoffa that night, as a "loyal" friend who was there to watch his back. Sheeran actually drove Hoffa to "the meet." When they arrived at the house where the meeting was to take place, Hoffa sensed something was amiss and bolted for the door. But Sheeran saw to it that he did not make it out of the room alive. Sheeran figuratively stabbed Hoffa in the back, and literally shot him twice behind the ear. It was a mob hit designed to keep Hoffa from returning to power. (All of this is according to Sheeran's interview.)

Often in the annals of organized crime it is a friend or trusted ally who whacks the intended victim. Children are always warned not to get in a car with strangers. But a Mafioso who is even remotely worried about his standing in the family should also be very hesitant about getting in a car with his best friend.

Sheeran was questioned shortly after the murder, but he pleaded the Fifth. He died at the age of eighty-three without making an official deathbed confession. Besides speaking off the record to Fox News, Sheeran collaborated with his lawyer on a book, but he never spoke to the authorities. Hoffa's family believes that Sheeran had a role in the murder but was not necessarily the triggerman. As of this writing, the house where Hoffa was allegedly killed has been torn apart by forensic experts, but the results have not been released. And although those traces of blood have been found, it is unclear whether thirty-year old bloodstains will yield any conclusive proof.

Under Siege 3: Steven Seagal versus the Mafia

This story is a very complicated one, with all sides blaming the others. It is far more complex than the plot of any Steven Seagal action flick, and it does not have the cathartic shoot-'em-up finale. This battle was settled in a more civilized fashion—the courtroom.

In the late 1990s, actor and martial-arts expert Steven Seagal was pals with a man named Julius Nasso, who had links to the Gambino crime family. According to published reports, they dressed alike and even had homes next to one another. Nasso was the executive producer of Seagal's early films—the good ones, the ones that made him a star. Then, as Seagal became more interested in Buddhism, his relationship with Nasso soured. Seagal's spiritual adviser told him it would be "bad karma" to continue to make violent movies. This of course led to a rift between the two men, culminating in 2002, when Nasso sued Seagal for breach of contract, claiming he backed out of a lucrative four-movie deal that would have netted the pair many millions of dollars.

A lawsuit is not the usual way the Mafia deals with a breach of contract. In fact, Seagal claims that Nasso had a couple of goons from the Gambino crime family threaten him. However, the action star did not pummel the leg breakers into submission—he told the FBI that before the lawsuit, he paid $700,000 to get the Mafia off his back. And the FBI's wiretap caught Nasso and other Mafiosi laughing about how they had scared the "tough guy" movie star and discussing what to do to him if he didn't pay up.

Nasso went on the offensive to besmirch Seagal's reputation by suggesting Seagal had been involved with the Mafia for years as more or less a hanger-on who was fascinated by the whole shady milieu. Seagal himself has painted a picture of himself as a man with a mysterious past. He has alluded to the fact that he was involved with the CIA and, as a Westerner studying martial arts in Japan, battled and defeated members of the notorious Yakuza. He has even declared that he is of Italian ancestry, though other records suggest this is not the case. What is a fact is that Seagal is a black belt and was a trainer to many celebrities, and this facilitated his entrée into the movies. He even accidentally broke Sean Connery's wrist while teaching him martial arts when the sparring became a little heated.

Nasso and several other Mafiosi are now behind bars. Seagal, though still a Buddhist, has continued making violent action pictures. And now he really is in legal trouble, having been accused of threatening a reporter who wrote about his connection with the Mafia. We hope he isn't heaping any more bad karma onto his soul.

The other Corleone family

Although the fictitious Corleone family of *Godfather* fame is practically seared into America's collective consciousness at this point, there was, in fact, a real-life, albeit lesser-known, Corleone crime family in Sicily. Its glory days were the 1980s and early 1990s. There was nothing noble, operatic, or Shakespearean about this crew. They make the fictional Corleone family seem like pussycats by comparison.

As those who saw *The Godfather II* know very well, Corleone is a town in Sicily. Don Vito Corleone was born Vito Andolini and his name was changed when he came to America through Ellis Island in New York Harbor. The immigration officials at the turn of the twentieth century, often baffled by the spelling and pronunciation of all the "foreign" names they encountered, frequently changed them while filling out the paperwork either through carelessness or contempt. Hence, Vito Andolini became Vito Corleone, renamed for his birthplace.

Two ruthless killers named Salvatore Riina and Bernardo Provenzano headed the real-life Corleone gang of Italy. Their initial claim to fame was the murder of their boss's rival, Michele Navarra, in 1958. Perfectionists, they fired 112 shots into the man's car, just to make sure that he would not live to drive another day. In 1963, Provenzano dropped off the face of the earth and remained missing for more than twenty years. Missing in the eyes of the law, that is. He was always lurking behind the scenes, pulling strings like a malevolent puppet master.

While Provenzano was the cool, level-headed one, Riina was the loose cannon. Where Provenzano was respected, Riina was hated. Both were feared. Riina is believed to have killed or ordered the killing of more than 800 men.

The Corleones were a barbaric crime family. They changed the modus operandi of the Mafia from subtle, shadowy dealings to in-your-face kidnappings and very public murders of elected officials and law enforcement personnel who were able to refuse the offers they made. This rampant violence led to a Mafia war in Sicily in the 1980s, a conflict in which the Corleone gang emerged victorious. They did so by murdering the leaders of rival families and offering incentives for the best and the brightest of the other camps to switch sides.

This brazen recklessness proved to be the Corleones' undoing, however. They took to the practice of eliminating enemies by blowing them up with car bombs. These very public bombings in the public streets created an outrage among the citizenry, which, in turn, forced the authorities to enact a massive crackdown. In fact, at one point when the American and Sicilian Mafias were discussing doing business on each other's turf, the American Mafia warned their counterparts that such behavior would not be tolerated in the United States.

Riina was arrested, tried, convicted, and sent up the river in 1993.

Italian prosecutors and politicians declared that the Mafia was defeated. Not so. Riina's partner Provenzano merely emerged from his undisclosed location and began to run things in a more low-key manner that involved a little less mayhem.

The Mafia, like the mythic bird Phoenix, always rises from its own ashes to wet its beak another day.

For every yin there is a yang, the spiritual among us maintain. It is also true that for every criminal there is a law enforcement official dedicated to putting the bad guy out of business. People have a fascination with the villains in movies, on television, and in real life. And it is true that the bad guys are often fun to watch and to read about. People respond to villains, from Shakespeare's Richard III to Darth Vader, on a visceral level.

Perhaps it is because these villains do things the rest of us would not, but in our secret hearts of darkness occasionally dare to fantasize about. Or maybe it's because characters like these have often

Part 5

Crime Fighters

"fallen from grace." They start out as decent members of society, but are somehow seduced by the Dark Side. Just look at Al Pacino's character in the *Godfather* movies. He begins as an idealistic young man, and by the end he has become all that he despises and swore he would never be. This is fascinating stuff, indeed.

Sure, the bad guys are fun to read about, but in the history of the Mafia, there have been crime fighters who are as equally intriguing as the bad guys. The individuals you'll read about in this section are an eclectic bunch, to say the least. These guys are not all angels—far from it. Nor are they all one-dimensional Dudley Do-Rights. They are heroic, flawed, stalwart, petty, and dedicated—and one of them may have even been a closet cross-dresser—but they all fought the Mafia and sought to eradicate its insidious presence on the American landscape. Well, all except for the alleged cross-dresser. His track record was lackluster, to say the least.

82

Purvis and Hoover

FBI Director J. Edgar Hoover's record for battling the Mafia was lackluster at best. He did, however, achieve national attention in the Depression-ravaged 1930s, when a different breed of gangster terrorized America's heartland. These criminals were not the slick and well-oiled cogs of elaborate La Cosa Nostra machinery. These were oddballs, outcasts, and misfits with colorful names like "Machine Gun" Kelly, "Pretty Boy" Floyd, "Baby Face" Nelson, "Ma" Barker, and Bonnie and Clyde. These notorious bank robbers cut a swath of mayhem across the Heartland.

As with the Mafia, the media often treated these cold-blooded killers like romantic modern-day Robin Hoods. Hoover was indignant, understandably so, and set the FBI on their trail. These men and women were not misunderstood decent folks who went bad because of the financial troubles of the Depression. Most decent people sought to provide for their families by finding work. These people were and are the real heroes. Stealing and killing do not a hero make.

The spectacular shoot-'em-ups that ensued between the feds and the crooks made FBI agents the celebrated Wyatt Earps of the day. In 1935, James Cagney even took a break from his usual gangster roles to star in a movie called *G-Men* (gangster-speak for the FBI—the *G* stands for *government*).

One of Hoover's star agents at the bureau during this time was the flamboyant Melvin Purvis. He is the agent who hunted down and killed the ruthless bank robber John Dillinger, with a little help from a shady dame who has gone down in history as the "Lady in Red."

Purvis went on to corner and kill Pretty Boy Floyd and Baby Face Nelson shortly after that. He was outshining Hoover, and J. Edgar deeply resented it. Hoover made life in the FBI so miserable for Purvis that he finally resigned. Not satisfied with that, Hoover followed Purvis's career with malevolent interest, often using his influence to prevent him from getting jobs in law enforcement. In 1960, Purvis shot himself with the same gun he had used to shoot down John Dillinger. He became a victim of J. Edgar Hoover's egotism and hubris.

In the 1970s, Purvis was the subject of a few TV movies, which, in part, restored his reputation, however melodramatically. He did not live to enjoy his fifteen minutes of acclaim as did another crime fighter of the day, Eliot Ness. And Ness had considerably more than the Warholian fifteen, although much of it came posthumously.

Eliot Ness's anticlimactic aftermath

Years after the height of his crime fighting, television and the movies made Eliot Ness and his story part of the fabric of American folklore. Unfortunately, Ness did not live to see his name become a household one. Ness wrote his memoirs in the 1950s but died shortly thereafter, so he didn't live to see the popularity of the book and the megapopularity of the TV show.

We have all heard the expression "Don't make a federal case out of it." This saying originated in Al Capone's Chicago. The Mafia did not want to tangle with the government. The power of federal law enforcement was formidable—it shined too much light on them. It was against the Mafia code to kill a cop and a very big no-no to whack a federal agent. But local cops were more easily bribed and intimidated.

Eliot Ness was a stalwart young federal agent working for the Bureau of Alcohol, Tobacco, and Firearms when he was assigned to the Chicago office and began his campaign against Al Capone. He and his elite corps were called "the Untouchables" because no one could bribe them. This set them apart from many of their brother officers at the federal level and on the Chicago police force.

Ness assembled a handpicked team of agents. He wanted his agents to be under thirty years of age and unmarried. It was a dangerous business, and he did not want to be a widow-maker. After extensive interviews, he settled on nine men. For the record, these were the real Untouchables: Marty Lahart, Sam Seager, Barney Cloonan, Lyle Chapman, Tom Friel, Joe Leeson, Paul Robsky, Mike King, and Bill Gardner.

During this time, the Chicago police force was corrupt and knew what was going on, but it turned a blind eye out of fear or bribery. Ness began by raiding Capone's breweries, which were often "hidden" in plain sight. The Untouchables also raided distilleries. Although most of the hard liquor consumed in Chicago was imported from elsewhere, the Capone mob made its own beer, and there were hundreds of breweries in the greater Chicagoland area. As Sean Connery's cop character tells Kevin Costner's Eliot Ness in the 1987 movie *The Untouchables*, "Everybody knows where the booze is. The problem isn't finding it. The problem is, who wants to cross Capone?"

Well, Ness was willing to cross Capone. It is estimated that Ness cost Capone more than $1 million in spilled beer by seizing and destroying his illegal breweries. Capone probably would not have cried over spilled milk, but that was a lot of lost loot in spilled brewski. Except gangsters don't cry—they kill you instead. Because bumping off Ness would make it a federal case and create myriad problems, Capone's first response was to try to bribe Ness and the Untouchables.

Capone offered Ness $2,000 a week to look the other way, but Ness turned down the bribe. Ness was making about $2,800 a year at the time. Ness, never shy of publicity and often accused of egomania, held a press conference to announce that he had turned down the bribe. (It was at this press conference that one of the newspapermen who covered the event coined the moniker the Untouchables.)

When the attempts at bribery failed, Capone later tried to kill Ness. Ness discovered a bomb under the hood of his car. On another occasion, gunshots were fired at him as he escorted a date back to her home, and he was almost the victim of a hit-and-run.

Despite his violent track record, Capone was ultimately brought down by his long history as a tax scofflaw. An investigation that was years in the making culminated with an indictment against Capone in 1931. He faced twenty-two counts of tax evasion, on top of the evidence Ness had gathered of several thousand violations of the Prohibition law. The tax case was judged the easiest to win, and Capone went to trial.

Capone had a couple of months before his trial began, but the jury had already been selected. Because his henchmen took that time to locate and bribe the jurors-to-be, Big Al walked into the courtroom quite confident. He got the shock of his life when the judge switched juries, bringing in twelve men from another trial. Capone was found guilty, fined $50,000, and sentenced to eleven years in prison. The reign of Al Capone was over.

Eliot Ness never became a law enforcement superstar after his success in Chicago. He bounced around in other assignments that were not as high profile. It is generally believed that another federal official,

J. Edgar Hoover, was envious of Ness's successes and did his best to sabotage his career. Eliot Ness was largely forgotten when he wrote his memoirs in the 1950s. He died soon thereafter at the age of fifty-four, and did not live to see his autobiography turned into a hit television series and later an Academy Award–winning feature film.

Turning a blind eye on the Mafia

J. Edgar Hoover was director of the FBI for almost fifty years. In that time he amassed detailed files on thousands of politicians, entertainers, and ordinary citizens. It is believed that the dirt he had on the revolving-door residents of the White House was sometimes used as blackmail, and was one of the ways he maintained job security.

In the 1920s Hoover was placed in charge of the newly formed General Intelligence Division of the Justice Department, and his career as a lawman began. It was here that Hoover began his lifetime obsession of amassing files on people. In these early days, his files mostly dealt with suspected "radical" groups. But what began as a necessary endeavor over the decades turned into nothing short of the unwarranted persecution of innocent individuals. Hoover fancied himself the final arbiter of what was considered radical and "anti-American," and the Hoover Files eventually included people like Bing Crosby and Rock Hudson—hardly rabid anarchists bent on toppling the government.

Hoover rose within the ranks of the Justice Department, seeking out and destroying communists and other radicals both real and imagined. His eyes were on his prize, his personal Holy Grail—directorship of the Bureau of Investigation, later called the Federal Bureau of Investigation. He achieved that goal in 1924 and remained in the position until his death in 1972.

Hoover, who liked to dress in white linen suits and had an avid interest in collectibles, was never seen in the company of women and had a longtime male companion, fellow FBI agent Clyde Tolson. They worked together and lived together. Naturally, the rumor mill dished gossip about Hoover's sexual tastes for decades. One mobster claimed to have seen a photograph of Hoover in women's clothing, dressed as a 1920s flapper. The photo has never surfaced.

Hoover, the intrepid lawman, keeper of the national dish and dirt, did not have an exemplary record as an antagonist of the Mafia. In fact, he repeatedly denied that an organized crime network existed in the United States. Hoover and his beloved bureau took a lot of heat in the court of public opinion and from the politicians in Washington, D.C., who wanted to know "what he knew and when he knew it," as they say in Washington. And if Hoover did not know anything about the Mafia, Congress wanted to know why. Eventually, Hoover engaged in some aggressive damage control with a program he called the Top Hoodlum Program.

But the fact remains that Hoover did sidestep the issue of organized crime throughout much of his career. His titanic ego might have been the reason for this stubborn denial. Conspiracy theorists may find more sinister reasons for his refusal to acknowledge the mob's existence. Whatever the reasons for his belief, it made Hoover either a willing or an unintentional accomplice in the Mafia's rapid growth and increased influence on the American landscape.

The theory that gives J. Edgar Hoover the benefit of the doubt postulates that he was afraid corruption would spread through the bureau if his agents had close contact with the Mafia. The Mafia would not have become as powerful as it did if not for the greed of law enforcement officials at the local and state levels. Hoover's rationale may have been to steer clear of the Mafia's seductive allure and concentrate on his favorite pursuits, tracking down real and suspected communists and indulging his voyeuristic interest in the sexual peccadilloes of others. Skeptics suggest that Hoover focused on easy targets to increase his crime-busting statistics, which would, in turn, enhance his acclaim and increase the likelihood of receiving additional funding for his bureau from Congress.

There is a line from *The Godfather* in which Don Barzini, tells his rival, Don Corleone, "After all, we are not communists," and in a twisted manner, the Mafia's leaders were participants in and advocates of the free enterprise system. Just like the CEOs of any big corporation, they were enthusiastic capitalists. There are those who suggest that Hoover saw them as ideological soul mates. The Mafia did not advocate the overthrow of the government and the American way of life. They were no threat to the status quo—in fact they thrived in the status quo.

It is reported that Hoover mingled with the Mafia. They were often at the same parties and social functions. Hoover loved gambling, especially on the horses, and this was, as we know, a main source of the Mafia's income. Hoover was often at the racetrack with his pal Clyde Tolson. He was publicly spotted betting at the $2 window, a seemingly innocuous pastime. But he had agents placing bets for him at the $100 window, because it would have ruined his reputation as Mr. Law and Order if the public found out he was a high-stakes gambler.

Or were the stakes really that high? Hoover got his betting "tips" from the notorious syndicated columnist Walter Winchell, who in turn got them from Mafia boss Frank Costello. In other words, Hoover was, whether he knew it or not, betting on fixed races. Hence, he was a big winner. Hoover may not have known it then, but he was being manipulated by the Mafia. However, if he did know about it, Mr. FBI was engaging in behavior punishable by imprisonment. When Hoover died in 1972, the Mafia was sorry to see him go. In the post-Hoover years, the FBI has been considerably more aggressive in its efforts to arrest and prosecute Mafia leaders.

85

Dewey defeats Lucky

Thomas Dewey was the Republican presidential candidate who ran against Harry S. Truman in 1948. His name is perhaps best known from a still photograph from that era that shows Truman holding up a prematurely released newspaper with the headline "DEWEY DEFEATS TRUMAN."

Dewey was a New York district attorney and later governor who prosecuted Lucky Luciano. He was also a politically ambitious man who used his mob convictions to further his political career. Thomas Dewey aggressively went after the prostitution racket in New York. Forty brothels were raided and 100 or so women were arrested. Many of the prostitutes told sad tales of their lives and their many abuses at the hands of the syndicate. Soon, Luciano had a large group of women spilling the beans to the law. Never mind the other rackets; Dewey compiled an airtight case against Luciano in the prostitution business alone. And this was enough to put him away.

Feeling the heat, Luciano decided to take in the waters at Hot Springs, Arkansas. This Southern Sin City was a prime vacation spot for the Capone mob. Luciano was caught in Hot Springs and taken back to New York City in a heavily guarded railroad car. And then the unthinkable happened: Lucky Luciano had been arrested and was put on trial. Even more astoundingly, he was convicted and sentenced to thirty to fifty years in the big house.

Ironically, one of Dewey's subsequent duties as governor was to pardon Luciano on the condition that he be deported to Italy. Dewey pardoned Luciano because the federal government wanted the Mafiosi's assistance in the war effort. Luciano had contacts in Sicily and Italy that, the government supposedly believed, could help the Allies with intelligence. The merits of this action are debatable. Although Luciano may have rendered some help during the war, the fact remains he was a dangerous man turned loose into the world to continue his nefarious behavior.

A tale of two brothers

A fascinating subplot in the life of Al Capone involves his long lost older brother, James Vincenzo, who left home at age sixteen in 1908, never to return. Young Al was eight at the time. James went way out west, joined a circus, mingled with Native Americans, and, like many Italian-Americans of the day, changed his name. He became Richard Hart.

Hart fought bravely in World War I. He was the only son in the

Capone family to see battle in the trenches. Though Al often claimed that he got his scar in the war, in reality, the angry brother of a woman Al insulted marked him with his famous wound (see number 56).

After the war, Richard Hart went back to the Midwest, married a local girl, started a family, and made Homer, Nebraska, his home. Ironically, he became a law enforcement officer and built a name for himself chasing moonshiners and keeping alcohol off Indian reservations. He even had a nickname: "Two Gun" Hart.

Al Capone's brother was a frontier lawman in the modern Wild West, and he spoke several Indian languages. He even served as a bodyguard for President Calvin Coolidge. Al Capone had a few other brothers who worked for him, but all had lost touch with their elder sibling. While Scarface Capone was committing murder and mayhem in the big city of Chicago, making his money through the manufacture and sale of illegal booze, his older brother was arresting bootleggers and confiscating stills a few hundred miles away.

Two Gun Hart and his family became close with members of the Sioux and Cheyenne Indian nations. He became fascinated with and empathetic to the culture of Native Americans. Brother Al was probably not a man of similar curiosity or depth. But they did both share a trait that the tribes of Israel called *chutzpah*.

In the 1940s Hart contacted his family and had a series of reunions with his brothers and his elderly mother. His wife and family were stunned to learn that he was the brother of Scarface Capone. He visited his notorious brother when Al was at the end of the line, suffering from the syphilis that would eventually kill him. He told the son that accompanied him to be cordial but not to get too close to Uncle Scarface. He did not want his kids to be influenced by their infamous uncle. This was unlikely, considering Al Capone's glory days were long behind him and the only thing ahead was continued mental and physical deterioration, followed by the big sleep.

Two Gun Hart died in 1953 with his wife and one of his sons at his side. He left a humble, wholesome, and quintessentially middle-America legacy, in stark contrast to that of his notorious younger brother.

The Little Flower

The early 1930s saw the end of Prohibition, a new president in the White House (Franklin Delano Roosevelt), and a new mayor in New York City. Fiorello LaGuardia, also known as the Little Flower (the English translation of his first name), had run as a reform candidate and was determined to use one of the planks of his political platform to whack the Mafia upside the head. It is possible that, as an Italian, he was particularly angry at the bad reputation the Mafia gave the rest of his people. Though most Italians had nothing to do with the Mafia, many non-Italians assumed that every neighbor whose name ended in a vowel must be affiliated in some way with La Cosa Nostra.

LaGuardia was a Republican mayor in a town with a strong Democratic political machine. He also had an Italian father and a Jewish mother. He was the personification of the changing face of New York City. The immigrant class, who came through Ellis Island as huddled masses yearning to breathe free, were taking their places as leaders in politics and assuming other positions of prestige and responsibility.

Around this time, Mafioso Frank Costello was in charge of the lucrative and very illegal slot-machine business in New York City. When crusading Mayor LaGuardia was elected in 1933, he began to make life difficult for the Mafia. Slot machines were seized and destroyed. LaGuardia had many a photo opportunity personally smashing slot machines for newsreel cameras. After the New York City slot bust, Huey Long, the former governor of Louisiana, approached Costello and agreed to act as broker in a deal to ship the surviving slot machines from New York to New Orleans, where they could be used for fun and profit. New Orleans Mafia kingpin Carlos Marcello made sure the machines were prominently displayed for public consumption in gambling joints, bars, and brothels in New Orleans and the surrounding communities.

LaGuardia's Mafia fighting didn't stop with slots, however. He also appointed Thomas Dewey as Special Prosecutor, and Dewey, in turn, became the bane of the existence of many a Mafioso, including Lucky

Luciano and Dutch Schultz. Although LaGuardia was a cute little man with a deceptively benign physiognomy (he resembled the comedian Lou Costello), he was a tough crime fighter. Nevertheless, LaGuardia is best known as the mayor who, during a newspaper strike, went on the radio and read comic strips to New York City's children.

Joe Petrosini: Hero cop

The early history of the Mafia in America certainly has its share of villains, but it also has its heroes. One of the most notable is Joe Petrosini, an Italian-American New York City police officer who took on the Mafia in both America and Italy.

Like many Italian-American crime fighters, it is likely that Petrosini took an even tougher stance against the mob because of the disgrace it brought on the reputation of fellow Italian-Americans. He probably felt the need to vindicate his people by fighting the insidious menace of this criminal minority of the Italian-American immigrants who came to America. Of course, just as the case is today, most of the Italian-Americans of Petrosini's time were hard-working folks who had no connection to the Mafia.

The main target of Petrosini's wrath was the New York chapter of the notorious Black Hand, the criminal organization that had come from Sicily. Its leader was a man called Lupo Saietta. In an investigation of Lupo's hideout, Petrosini uncovered the remains of more than sixty bodies, all victims of the Black Hand. The exact number was hard to specify, since the bodies had been hacked to pieces. In spite of this wealth of evidence, Lupo beat the rap. Petrosini was incensed and more determined than ever to bring the Black Hand to justice.

Meanwhile, Petrosini made lieutenant on the force and was put in charge of the "Italian Squad." These were an elite corps of Italian-American cops whose mandate was to infiltrate the Mafia. This unit succeeded in deporting more than 500 Mafiosi.

Petrosini was very successful on his home turf. Sadly, his luck changed when he took his crusade abroad. In 1909, he went to Sicily as part of a joint American-Sicilian, anti-Mafia task force. He was looking for evidence against Sicilian Mafiosi who were wanted in the States, and he conducted background checks on suspected gangsters. His main nemesis was one Vito Cascio Ferro. Petrosini had driven Ferro out of New York and down to New Orleans, but now Ferro was back in Sicily and had achieved the exalted position of *capo di tutti capi* (boss of all bosses).

Acting on an anonymous tip from an informant who had details about Ferro's activity, Petrosini went to the scheduled meeting place in a public square and was shot dead by three men. Petrosini's body was returned to New York. Among his personal effects were some clothes, a gold watch, and $12.40. His widow received a pension from the police department and friends took up a collection for the widow and orphans of this fallen hero. His funeral was one of the largest New York City had ever seen. More than 200,000 citizens turned out for the five-and-a-half-hour funeral procession through Manhattan.

The French connection

From World War II through the 1960s, Marseilles, France, was one of several cities where clandestine laboratories refined morphine base into heroin. In the 1950s, the Mafia began to shut down the Sicilian drug-producing labs and contract the work out to the Corsican crime families. Corsica is an island in the Mediterranean Sea, and Marseilles is a port city in the south of France. It is the port from which the French imperialists left to seek their fortunes in North Africa and Southeast Asia. The city has an international flavor, like most great metropolises with active sea commerce and busy docks. During the 1950s, it became a fertile breeding ground for a criminal element, just as New York City and New Orleans were and are for the American Mafia. French pulp fiction portrays Marseilles the way American writers of hardboiled crime fiction treat Chicago of the 1920s.

In the case of Marseilles, the local villains were the Corsican gangsters. The Corsican mob has always lacked the elaborate organization of the rest of the Mafia. Comprised of close-knit and insular clans who worked together for the greater evil, the Corsican mob has a track record of working for the highest bidder. The Americans, on occasion, have employed these Mafiosi. It is generally accepted that during the 1950s the CIA paid the Corsican mob to break striking communist members of European labor unions. The Corsican Mafiosi's association with the CIA made them an extremely powerful crime family and, in effect, made Marseilles the largest heroin producer in the Western world through the 1960s.

In the late 1940s, Meyer Lansky made a trip to Europe, securing the services of the Corsican mob while he was there. To avoid IRS scrutiny, Lansky established the clandestine financial network for organized crime activities that involved Swiss bank accounts. Swiss banks prided themselves on protecting the anonymity of their depositors by issuing numbered, not named, accounts and by fiercely guarding the identity of their clients. This kept the Mafia's finances hidden from inquisitive American authorities, who were eager to freeze or seize their assets. Eventually, however, Meyer Lansky bought his very own bank in Geneva to eliminate the middlemen.

Meyer Lansky's European jaunt also took him to Rome to see his old friend Luciano, and then on to France to negotiate with the Corsicans. A deal was struck, and in short order, Marseilles became the heroin-producing capital of Europe and the major supplier of heroin to the United States.

"Popeye" Doyle, played by Gene Hackman in the movie *The French Connection*, was based on real-life detective Eddie Egan, the man who, along with his partner Sonny Grosso, put a dent in the French connection with what was, at that time, the largest drug bust in New York City history. These two average Joe cops followed a labyrinthine trail through the streets of New York, working long hours, often on their own time. Their story was made into a book and then an Academy Award–winning film. Heroic as it was on a personal level, the "war on drugs" appears to be a never-ending story without a satisfactory conclusion.

RICO

In the early 1980s, the U.S. government was aggressively going after the heads of the five New York families. These Mafiosi were being prosecuted under charges that came to be called RICO (Racketeer Influenced and Corrupt Organizations). Paul Castellano learned that he was going to be indicted in at least two RICO cases, but John Gotti saved the taxpayers' money and had Big Paulie whacked first.

Gotti was acquitted again on more than one RICO charge before finally being convicted. As is often the case with bureaucracies (in organized crime and the legitimate world), there were rivalries and infighting among the prosecution attorneys and the FBI agents who brought them the evidence. Hence, for a time, Gotti was briefly called "the Teflon Don," because no charges would stick to him.

But ultimately it became clear that even if the charges weren't sticking to Gotti, other Mafiosi weren't getting off so easy. In 1981, after decades of seeming invulnerability, Carlos Marcello, the don of the New Orleans Mafia, was found guilty of violating the RICO law.

Racketeering, which includes extortion, bribery, loan sharking, murder, illegal drug sales, and prostitution, are certainly the Mafia's bread and butter. A Mafia kingpin need not necessarily have committed these crimes himself in order to be prosecuted under RICO. He is treated like a corrupt CEO and prosecuted for incidents that transpired under his watch, with his full knowledge and consent.

Incidentally, the RICO Act is not exclusively applicable to the Mafia. Many "legitimate" businesses that have engaged in questionable business practices have been charged under the RICO Act. There are also criminal and civil distinctions to be made. The government can prosecute in a criminal case, and a private citizen can sue for damages in a civil action.

Motorcycle gangs, gangsta rappers, terrorist organizations, and anti-abortion activists have all been prosecuted under the RICO Act. The latest group to incur the wrath of RICO is e-mail spammers. Annoying as e-mail spam can be, it is hardly in the same league as the Mafia. Nevertheless, in the eyes of the government, those annoying popup ads that surreptitiously download spyware are on par with the Mafia and should be punished accordingly.

Witnesses for the prosecution

The Witness Protection Program has become the last refuge of many a Mafia rat. Some informants go into deep cover and remain there; others cannot give up their wicked ways and get into brand-new trouble under their new identities.

The reason that prosecutors have always had a problem getting convictions against the Mafia is that often their star witnesses are bribed, intimidated, or worse. For example, witnesses always had a funny way of losing their memories when questioned about their relationship with John Gotti. The *New York Post*, always good for a clever headline, once ran "I FORGOTTI" on their front page about one such witness who neglected to take his ginkgo biloba. In order to ensure that its witnesses lived long enough to testify, the government had to keep them in protective custody. This was not good enough, however, because the Mafia has a long memory and has gone after witnesses long after their testimonies put a hood behind bars. As a result, the Witness Protection Program was created.

It was called the Witness Security Program when it was enacted by the Organized Crime Control Act of 1970 and amended to the Witness Protection Program by the Comprehensive Crime Control Act of 1984. According to government statistics, the program has relocated and given new identities to more than 7,500 witness and 9,500 of their family members since its inception. Those in the program receive a new name with the appropriate documentation (birth certificate, new social security number, etc.) and are provided with health care, job training, housing, and an income until they get settled and established in their new locale.

The government also claims that it has secured a conviction rate of 89 percent against those who were prosecuted based on testimony provided by witnesses in the program. It also maintains that no one who has followed the rules to the letter has come to harm while in the program. But not everyone does, as you can imagine. The government cites that 17 percent of those in the program return to a life of crime under their new identities. There is no "diplomatic immunity" pass for those in the program, as Henry Hill and Sammy "The Bull" Gravano can confirm. These two rascals engaged in illegal activity in their new lives and summarily found themselves boiling in a new pot of hot water. You can take the punk out of the Mafia, but you can't always take the Mafia out of the punk.

The taxman cometh

Most people with even a casual knowledge of the Mafia have heard of the celebrated crime fighter Eliot Ness, but far fewer may know about a man named Elmer Irey. He was a contemporary of Ness, and was perhaps even more instrumental in bringing down the mighty Al Capone.

Elmer Irey was an accountant—a mild-mannered profession in the minds of most. Those of us who have had dealings with the taxman at either the state or local level know he can be a mean SOB, indeed— someone you should not mess with or take lightly. The taxman has the full weight of the powers-that-be behind him, and if you cross him he can descend upon your head like the sword of Damocles or the proverbial ton of bricks. And this is what happened to Al Capone.

The story is proof that, although you can often get away with murder, you can rarely, if ever, get away with not paying your taxes. Elmer

Irey was chief of the U.S. Treasury Enforcement Branch and head of the IRS Special Intelligence Unit. From his office in Washington, D.C., Irey orchestrated Capone's downfall. He had two field agents infiltrate the Capone organization to follow the paper trail of the Mafia's "creative accounting" practices. Once identified, Irey, along with a government lawyer named George E. Q. Johnson, built the case against Capone that culminated in an eleven-year prison sentence.

Irey and his team were called the "silent investigators." They practiced what is known as forensic accounting long before that term even existed. Just as a forensic pathologist (recall classic television's *Quincy* and today's various *CSI* incarnations) solves crimes through medical and scientific investigations, so too the forensic accountant solves crimes by immersing himself in numbers. Who says accounting is not a glamorous, and sometimes dangerous, profession?

The Kennedys

Despite their indirect links to Mafiosi, John and Robert Kennedy, sons of privilege and public servants, were also crime fighters in their own right. Armchair psychologists of the Freudian variety may suggest that they were acting out an Oedipal impulse to destroy their father. Patriarch Joseph Kennedy was a bootlegger during Prohibition who did business with the Mafia on a regular basis during the course of his long life. Is a "businessman" who does business with gangsters not himself a gangster? The patrician Kennedys didn't think so. There was some good old-fashioned denial going on up there in Massachusetts.

Both JFK and RFK were on the congressional committee investigating teamster boss Jimmy Hoffa and his role in alleged Mafia corruption of that union. The swaggering and confident Hoffa saw the Kennedys as uppity pipsqueaks. In fact, charges of political opportunism were leveled at the Kennedys on more than one occasion during their careers. Liberal Democrat Robert Kennedy was an ally of the right-wing senator Joseph McCarthy, the man who is synonymous with "witch hunt" because of his anticommunist congressional hearings in the 1950s. It is worth noting that, although McCarthy was not a particularly nice fellow and many innocent lives were ruined during the dark days of blacklisting, declassified documents from the former Soviet Union make it plain that there were communist infiltrators in the U.S. government and in Hollywood during that time. One report alleges that Josef Stalin personally sent a hit team to dispatch John Wayne. The Russians knew the value of propaganda, and there is no more effective propaganda machine than Hollywood.

Robert Kennedy had a history of taking on the Mafia, and he wanted to continue the crusade as Attorney General. This is not without irony, because there is strong evidence that John Kennedy might not have been elected without the Mafia's help. It is generally accepted that old Joe Kennedy prevailed upon Frank Sinatra to ask his Mafia pals to use their influence to swing the vote in West Virginia, a must-win state for Kennedy in the 1960 Democratic primary. The Mafia control of labor unions influenced the voting among the rank-and-file members and secured a victory for Kennedy over his challenger, Hubert Humphrey.

Robert Kennedy was not afraid of the infamous J. Edgar Hoover, lifetime head of the FBI. RFK forced Hoover to ratchet up his efforts against organized crime, and Hoover was livid that this cocky young rich kid did not defer to him. Ultimately, the Kennedys' arrogance and recklessness worked against them, and when Hoover saw an opportunity to remind them who had the power, he did not hesitate (see number 46).

After John Kennedy's assassination in 1963, Robert Kennedy resigned as attorney general to run for one of New York State's seats in the United States Senate. He, like Hillary Rodham Clinton, was not from New York, but saw being a senator from the Empire State as a springboard to further his political ambitions. Unfortunately, RFK met the same tragic fate as his brother when he was struck down by an assassin's bullets in 1968 during his run for the Democratic presidential nomination.

94

The Kefauver Committee

Carey Estes Kefauver was a Democratic congressman and later a senator from the state of Tennessee. Beginning in May of 1950, for fifteen months he was the chairman of the Special Committee on Organized Crime in Interstate Commerce. This organization has since become known simply as the Kefauver Committee. A road show committee that visited fourteen cities and questioned 800 witnesses, it also became a television-ratings winner long before the days of twenty-four-hour cable news networks. In fact, the medium of television was only in its infancy at this time.

From March 12 to March 20, 1951, the committee set up shop in New York City. More than fifty witnesses were questioned, including mob boss Frank Costello. This was the first time most Americans had ever heard the word "Mafia." It was also several years before the Apalachin fiasco; thereafter, "Mafia" became a household word. When the combative Kefauver asked Costello why he should be considered a good American, the Mafioso shrugged and quipped that he paid his taxes. This was, of course, most likely perjury.

When the Kefauver Committee rolled into New Orleans, Bayou Boss Carlos Marcello was called in for questioning. Marcello pleaded the Fifth 152 times during his questioning. He was, essentially, admitting that he was guilty but was unwilling to incriminate himself by answering. His smug demeanor also earned the committee's ire, and he was cited for contempt, but the six-month jail sentence was later overturned on appeal. Kefauver was outraged and publicly announced his desire to see Marcello deported back to Italy.

Kefauver's committee was largely responsible for defeating attempts to legalize gambling in Massachusetts, Montana, Arizona, and California. It also heightened public awareness about the criminals lurking in those states. And it led to the formation of the McClellan Commission, which was even more successful in its prosecution of the Mafia.

Kefauver, a Southern senator, was nevertheless sympathetic to the civil rights movement. He ran for vice-president under Adlai Stevenson in 1956, in an unsuccessful bid to oust popular incumbent Dwight Eisenhower. He died in 1963.

Waste management

The waste management business is the last racket the Mafia seems to have controlled with an iron grip. It is not surprising that Tony Soprano gives this as his line of work.

The Mafia had a monopoly on the private trash removable business in New York City and the surrounding areas beginning in the 1950s. Businesses large and small had to pay the exorbitant rates, lest they face intimidation, or worse. The examples are legion. One small business owner, who had just opened his pet shop in Yonkers, New York, was approached by a Mafioso, and this brave but foolhardy entrepreneur threw the man out of his place of business. Later that evening, a garbage can was thrown through his store window. After that, the pet-shop owner played ball.

This corruption ended in 1995 through the efforts of an Irish-American New York City cop named Rick Cowan. He spent several years undercover, masquerading as an Italian-American named Dan Benedetto, claiming he was from a company called Chambers Paper Fibres Corp., a paper recycling business. Known as Operation Wasteland, Cowan's elaborate sting operation showed that major corporations, small businesses, printers, and scrap-paper generators were all subject to price gouging and rigged bidding by the Mafia, which was operating behind front companies with names like the Greater New York Waste Paper Association, the Association of Trade Waste Removers of Greater New York, the Kings County Trade Waste Association, and the Queens County Trade Waste Association.

Cowan/Benedetto wore a wire and had his office bugged, and he taped hundreds of hours of conversations with Mafiosi who used threats and intimidation to make him get with their program. He ultimately blew the lid off this crime cartel. Seventeen men from twenty-three companies and trade associations were indicted in 1995. With the return of honest business practices and healthy competition, New York businesses saw their waste management bills drop by as much as 90 percent.

After working closely with the goodfellas who knew him as Benedetto for years, Rick Cowan had to meet them again in the courtroom, as he testified against them under his real name and occupation. As of this writing, Cowan is still on the force, yet he will live the rest of his life with a target on his chest. Cowan was responsible for sending seventy-two Mafiosi to jail, and for bringing down a $1.5 billion-a-year enterprise. The Mafia is not likely to forget that anytime soon.

Burton Turkus: The crusading DA

Burton Turkus was the Brooklyn district attorney who was instrumental in bringing down Murder, Incorporated. As explained elsewhere in this book, Murder, Inc., was the Mafia Commission's assassination squad. These were not guns for hire. They acted only under the Commission's orders, and their work took them all over the country. Though they were mostly Jewish gangsters who operated out of a candy store in the Brownsville section of Brooklyn, their tentacles reached anywhere the Commission felt they were "needed."

Later in life, Burton Turkus took great pains to make this point. Murder, Inc., was not a "Brooklyn thing." It was a national organization. Turkus coordinated his investigations with law enforcement agencies from sea to shining sea and all across the fruited plain.

The investigation began when his staff inadvertently discovered a vast Mafia conspiracy while looking into another unrelated matter. Turkus sent seven men to the electric chair as a result of his successful prosecution of Murder, Inc., including the group's ringleader, Louis Lepke. The Mad Hatter, Albert Anastasia, who escaped conviction for his Murder, Inc., activities, succeeded Lepke, but he was ultimately killed by his own in the celebrated barbershop hit in 1957 (see number 72).

In Burton Turkus's colorfully written memoir, *Murder, Inc.: The Story of "The Syndicate"* he describes the lengthy investigation and the various modes of murder employed by the hit men. These were not just ham-handed goons who would come at their targets with guns blazing. Shooting the victims was still the most commonly used method, but strangulation and impalement with an ice pick were also popular. Many victims were dropped into quicklime pits, and others were buried alive. Some were cremated, and some were tied up with ropes in such a way that their own struggles to break free strangled them. Many times, the victim's "punishment" fit the offense. An owner of a business that had mob slot machines was believed to be less than honest in his monthly payoffs, so he was tied to one of the heavy machines and dumped in a lake. Since murder was their business day in, day out, perhaps the members of Murder, Inc., felt the need to be creative in order to break up the monotony.

Turkus was the first to admit that his big break in the case came when Murder, Inc., collapsed from within because of an informant. The most famous informant was a hood named Abe "Kid Twist" Reles. He was so nicknamed because of his penchant for strangulation. He turned states' evidence and helped to crack the Commission's killing machine. He also fell out of a window while in police custody. It was ruled a suicide, but was more likely a mob murder in cooperation with some corrupt cops. Reles became known as the canary who could sing, but couldn't fly.

Peter Falk played Reles in the 1960 movie *Murder, Inc.*, based on Burton Turkus's book of the same name. Turkus even had a cameo role in the film. He died in 1982.

97

Falcone and Borsellino: Italian heroes

Giovanni Falcone and Paolo Borsellino were two Sicilian judges who specialized in Mafia prosecutions. Unfortunately, the two paid for it with their lives. In Sicily, judges, or magistrates as they are also known, are more like district attorneys and prosecutors than the American notion of a judge—someone who presides impartially over a trial. They are just two of the many Italian and Italian-American heroes who fell in the line of duty doing battle with their crooked kinsmen.

Falcone and Borsellino were boyhood friends who grew up in a poor section of Palermo, a city in Sicily. From their youth, they were well aware of the Mafia's insidious influence over Sicily, and anywhere else it set up shop. As adults, they both strove to eradicate this unsightly stain from their beloved country.

Their investigative technique made them unique among Mafia prosecutors, perhaps because they were genuinely interested in getting rid of the gangsters. Many others in politics and law enforcement were in collusion with the Mafia. Falcone and Borsellino "followed the money," tracking down Mafia bank accounts and financial activities. (Elmer Irey was doing same thing against Al Capone in America during the 1930s and the fact that Sicilian law enforcement did not think of this until the late 1980s is an indication that they did not really want to pursue the matter aggressively.) Many of the other law enforcement officials did not appreciate Falcone and Borsellino's efforts, and the two men were frequently the targets of gossip, rumor, and hostility.

The Sicilian Mafia, specifically the Corleone gang, under the leadership of Salvatore Riina, was feeling the pressure and fought back in a way the American Mafia would not have.

In 1992, Falcone, his wife (also a judge), and their bodyguards were killed when a bomb destroyed their car. Less than two months later, a car bomb destroyed an entire government office building in downtown Palermo, killing Borsellino and many others. The resulting public outcry forced a crackdown on the Mafia that led to the arrest and conviction of Riina and many others. In a change of policy in the Sicilian prison system, Riina and other Mafia bosses were isolated from the inmate population, and their visitation rights were severely restricted. This was done to prevent the Mafia leaders from continuing to call the shots from behind bars, something the American Mafia dons had a long tradition of doing while serving time.

Palermo Airport is now called the Falcone-Borsellino Airport in honor of these two martyrs to the never-ending war against the Mafia.

The McClellan Commission

The McClellan Commission, formally known as the Senate Select Committee on Improper Activities, was in existence from 1957 to 1963. Its most famous members were the Kennedy brothers, Jack and Bobby. John Kennedy was a senator at the time of its formation, and Robert was the commission's chief counsel. The brothers continued their crusade as the president and attorney general of the United States.

The seeds of conspiracy were planted in these years, since both men were on a commission that went after the Mafia, and both were assassinated in their prime by so-called "lone gunmen," who probably weren't very lonely at all.

The list of Mafiosi the McClellan Commission investigated includes almost all the usual suspects of gangland's golden age. New Orleans crime king Carlos Marcello, years after displaying his contempt to the Kefauver Committee, was equally disdainful of the McClellan Commission. The Kennedy brothers questioned Marcello, who was, no doubt, well aware that their father, Joe Kennedy, made his fortune in the bootlegging business during Prohibition. He didn't think that these preppie pipsqueaks could do him much harm. He had not anticipated one of them becoming president and making the other the attorney general. Just as he did when questioned by the Kefauver Committee, Marcello pled the Fifth over and over again and made no attempt to hide his scorn of the Kennedy brothers.

The most famous Tampa Mafioso, Santo Trafficante Jr., also appeared before the commission. He succeeded his father in the family business and had a very long and successful career, without ever going to jail or getting whacked. His claim to fame among conspiracy buffs is that his name comes up in the many theories about the assassination of President John F. Kennedy. Both he and Carlos Marcello were named in a congressional investigation into the Kennedy assassination in the 1970s.

The committee also took on teamster boss Jimmy Hoffa, and his testimony incriminated him to the tune of ten years behind bars. He was pardoned and tried to make a comeback, although it is alleged that the Mafia decided this was a bad idea and ended his plans with a bang, not a whimper. He disappeared in 1975, and his remains have never been found.

Joe Valachi's testimony was a television-ratings winner. Colorful and lurid, but perhaps not all that effective for the prosecution, Valachi helped fuel the American public's fascination with the Mafia, but his breaking of the vaunted omerta vow did not result in any significant convictions.

Unholy alliance

There is a scene in a corny Disney movie called *The Rocketeer* that paints a somewhat favorable picture of the Mafia. Set in the 1940s, the story concerns a young man who finds a top-secret government jet pack, and uses it to become a flying superhero. Everyone is after him—the military, the Nazis, and the Mafia. At one point the Mafia boss, upon realizing that the man he is working with is a German spy, proudly declares that he is an American and fights side by side with the FBI against the Nazi spies.

Alas, life is no longer like that, if indeed it ever was.

Today's Mafia has no compunction about forming allegiances with the new enemy—Islamic fundamentalist terrorists. Pierluigi Vigna, Italy's anti-Mafia prosecutor, recently revealed that the crime family in Naples, Italy (known as the Camorra; see number 3), has chosen to do business with Muslim extremists post 9/11. According to Vigna's reports, the Mafia has been giving the terrorists weapons in exchange for drugs. These weapons are likely to be used against Europeans, Israelis, Arabs, and possibly Americans. Vigna believes this unholy alliance may have been formed when a member of the Mafia converted to Islam while in prison and established contacts in the terrorist underworld.

The Mafia has never been a band of angels. Mafiosi have always been a self-serving bunch, more interested in money than morals. But it is hard to believe that the old guard from back in the day would make a deal with Islamic terrorists. They probably would have at least had the foresight to know that the Mafia would hardly prosper if the United States were under the constant threat of terrorist attack. Lucky Luciano, Meyer Lansky, and the rest of the gang knew that America was the last, best hope for the Mafia. They thought of themselves as capitalist businessmen, not too different from their "legitimate" doppelgangers in the business world, who take part in their fair share of skullduggery and corruption, though they probably don't commit murder on a regular basis.

"America's Mayor"

Another crime fighting New York City mayor in the tradition of Fiorello LaGuardia is Rudy Giuliani. And, like LaGuardia, Giuliani is an Italian-American who took on the Italians in the Mafia. During one of Giuliani's terms as mayor, it came to light that his father once did a sixteen-month stretch in Sing Sing before Rudy was born. If Rudy knew of this as a young man, perhaps it fueled his passion for law enforcement, just as the Kennedy sons took on the Mafia in an attempt to expiate the sins of their father.

Before becoming mayor, Rudy made a name for himself as a prosecutor. He was chief of the Narcotics Unit in the U.S. Attorney's office before he was thirty. He rose within the ranks in Washington to become associate attorney general, which is the third-highest position in the Department of Justice. There he supervised all federal law enforcement agencies, the Bureau of Corrections, the Drug Enforcement Agency, and the U.S. Marshals.

In 1983, he returned to his beloved New York, when he was appointed U.S. attorney for the southern district of New York. From this position, he aggressively took on the Mafia. Giuliani's overall record is impressive: 4,152 convictions, with a mere 25 reversals.

Although he ran for mayor and was narrowly defeated in 1989, he returned in 1993 and won. He served two terms as mayor. In those years he continued to take on the Mafia, successfully chipping away at its insidious influence over the private garbage removal business (waste management to the Sopranos) and the historic Fulton Fish Market.

The complex Giuliani has a love-hate relationship with the Mafia. He loves the movie *The Godfather*, and often regales those around him with a Marlon Brando imitation of dubious merit. He quotes from the movie often, and it is alleged that he made his staff watch the film more than once. Yet he harrumphed when *Time* magazine included Lucky Luciano as one of the top 100 American business leaders. The magazine cited Luciano's role in the formation of the Commission and his efforts to make the Mafia structure mirror its more legitimate counterparts.

Although he did plenty to chase out crime and clean up the Big Apple, Rudy will forever be known to most New Yorkers, and non-New Yorkers, as the man who remained a tower of strength when the Twin Towers were toppled by al-Qaeda terrorists on 9/11. As of this writing he is in the private sector, but don't be surprised if he has returned to the political arena by the time you are reading this book.

Are you doing business with the Mafia?

You may not think there is much you can do to thwart the activities of the Mafia. And if you could, you might not want to get involved with it in any capacity, lest the fate of Luca Brasi befall you and you find yourself sleeping with the fishes. But if you like pizza and cheap electronics, you are, in your own small way, in bed with the mob.

The Mafia is the dark side of the American Dream. In many ways, it is the embodiment of the distasteful underbelly of the capitalist, free-market economy. Crime families have not fared well under dictatorships. Fascist dictator Benito Mussolini waged war against the Sicilian Mafia, and a dastardly Russian Mafia emerged after the fall of the Soviet Union. This is not to say that the dictatorships are on the right track. Everyone suffers under a totalitarian regime. Freedom is a memory, and dissenters are dispatched with cruel finality.

The Mafia knows quite well that it is a mirror image of its more legitimate counterparts, those offices in the steel and glass high-rises of America's urban centers. Meyer Lansky once said that the Mafia was bigger than U.S. Steel. And Mafiosi ironically called themselves the "captains of industry" during their halcyon heyday.

The Mafia tries to influence many businesses, inserting itself in order to wet its beak. For years the Fulton Fish Market in Manhattan was under mob control. Anyone who shopped in local fish stores or dined in Manhattan was in league with the Mafia. And this does not only apply to yuppies eating guppies in tony New York City restaurants. The denizens of the neighborhood pizza joint are also consuming Mafia product. It is believed that the mob has the concession on the pizza cheese supply business. This does not apply to Pizza Hut or Dominos, but it does apply to the mom-and-pop, small pizzerias in large urban centers.

If you like to play pinball or get your soft drinks and candy from a vending machine, you are also doing business with the Mafia. Rumor has it they control these operations as well. And, of course, when you put those cheap batteries in that inexpensive Walkman you bought off a street merchant, you know in your heart that it "fell off the back of a truck." And you know who was there to catch it—your friendly neighborhood Mafioso.

Index